1986

The Innovators

The Innovators

16 Portraits of the Famous And the Infamous

Jay Robert Nash

REGNERY GATEWAY

Library of Congress Catalog Card Number 81-85515
ISBN 0-89526-658-X

Regnery Gateway
360 West Superior Street
Chicago, Illinois 60610

This book is to the memory of my dear friend,
Bob Abel

Go far; come near;
You still must be
The center of your own small mystery.
   —Walter de la Mare

Contents

Preface

The idea for this work—a collection that would involve those whose lives and careers, inseparable for the most part, epitomize the individual at his or her rugged best—has long been in the mind of the author. Most of those interviewed or profiled in this work are artists of the highest level in the fields of writing, painting, architecture, filmmaking, photography, jazz, albeit two arch criminals are also included to present "the other side of the curtain," as Blasco Ibañez called it, minds of high intellect that chose, for one reason or another, to pursue the career and fate of the miscreant.

Though all of the lives and careers herein are varied, there is a universal statement running throughout the book that emphasizes the singlemindedness of each and every individual, from Alfred Hitchcock, who doggedly worked his way through the film industry's odd jobs to become one of the greatest film directors in motion picture history, to the zealous architect Frank Lloyd Wright who, at the first hint of success (with Louis Sullivan) struck boldly, if not blindly out on his own to establish a style that revolutionized American architecture. The dedication to self-expression of

both these great artists, as with all others profiled, was unrelenting. And that self-expression brought forth an astounding and enlightening creativity that changed international perspectives.

Change is the key to these innovators. In literature Hemingway changed the concept of the short story and the novel, fusing journalism and creative thought, offering a stubborn style, as did Faulkner, that, at first, made them pariahs in the literary establishment. To accomplish that change, at least for themselves in the gradual acceptance of their work, these writers endured critical condemnation, and, in the case of Faulkner, near poverty.

The greatest living portrait photographer, Yousuf Karsh, adopted an identical attitude as a youth, leaving a comfortable position to strike out on his own, irrespective of hardship, to develop a style of portrait photography wholly unlike anything that had been seen before.

In the field of jazz, saxophonist Lawrence Bud Freeman is recognized today as a master, but only after decades of persevering through fads, big bands, and revisionist critics. He has kept intact what he refers to as "this little thing I do," his way of playing, his inimitable style, begun with the Austin High Gang in the early 1920s when that embryonic expression was first termed "Chicago Style." Freeman's music is indelibly *his,* alone and distinct; the jazz aficionado can pick out a Freeman tune from a thousand unlabeled records.

If there is a common philosophy shared by all presented in this book it is most certainly capsuled in Shakespeare's, "This above all—to thine own self be true . . . ." And, oddly enough, that lofty ideal applies even to the two stellar underworld figures presented herein, Joseph "Yellow Kid" Weil and Willie "The Actor" Sutton, malefactors who conned and robbed, yet had their own stern credos of conduct which they rigidly held to in their dubious professions.

Unrelenting loyalty to an idea, particularly one unpopular or utterly foreign to society, threatens the innovator with devastating rejection. Yet those artists interviewed and profiled in this collection took that conscious risk, for the most part, determined to spend their lives for the ideas their talents produced; a small and

Author Jay Robert Nash with (top) Alfred Hitchcock, (middle) Yousuf Karsh, and (bottom) Bud Freeman. (Freeman photo by Cathy Anetsberger)

valiant lot, as ever, in a world steadily shrinking from the thought of individual performance, courage, and excellence. With the exception of the underworld figures, the risks these gifted persons took proved worthwhile, beyond the gradual embrace of acceptance, to themselves and their work.

Selecting from dozens of articles published in the last 20 years, the author has attempted to present these innovators, either in short glimpses or long looks, through the expression of their immeasurable talents and, most important, their considerable humanity. The humanity, after all, is at the very hot core of the talent and the idea of the person. Here, the lava gushes from that hot core; it burns the memory, it fires the mind.

I would like to thank my research associate, Cathy Anetsberger, and my typist, Sandy Horeis, for all their wonderful help in the preparation of this work. Although most of the graphics employed herein come from the author's collection, I am indebted to the following for supplemental graphics: Bill Kelly of Wide World, Chicago; Cinemabilia of New York; Carol Kelm, Oak Park, Illinois Historical Society; Don Kalec of the Frank Lloyd Wright Home and Studio of Oak Park, Illinois; and the Chicago Historical Society.

Alfred Hitchcock/
A Quiet Interview
With Terror

London-born (on August 13, 1899), Alfred Joseph Hitch-cock was the third and last child of a middle-class grocer. He grew up with strict rules and the proper amount of fear—when Hitchcock was five, his father had him locked behind bars in a local jail for a short time, just so that he would know "what to expect" if he ever got into serious trouble, a trau-matic experience to be sure and one that never left Hitch-cock's mind. As a result of that "lock-up" the film director was forever afterward terrified of policemen. So deep was that fear that Hitchcock refused to learn how to drive a car; he was afraid that he might be stopped for some driving of-fense and have to confront a policeman, or so he later insisted.

Hitchcock took his first job in 1918 in a small advertising firm. After a brief training in engineering drawing and draft-ing, he became a technical clerk at the W. T. Henley Telegraph Company, manufacturers of electric cables. The firm encour-aged and paid for social activities thought to benefit its em-ployees. One of these was ballroom dancing and Hitchcock

Hitchcock: "Do you know what sludge is? It's half-decomposed flesh."

1

the clerk was taught dancing by a Mr. Graydon whose daughter, Edith, would, in 1922, become the central figure in London's most sensational murder case, the Thompson-Bywaters killing. Hitchcock never forgot this case and his own link to the personalities involved. He avidly followed the trial and, decades later, could rattle off the court testimony by heart. (Edith and her lover, Frederick Bywaters, were executed for the killing of Edith's husband, Percy Thompson; many believed Edith Graydon Thompson to be innocent.) There is little doubt that this case not only fascinated Hitchcock but was an early influence in his decision to specialize in *film noir* as a director.

As a youngster, Hitchcock occupied much of his time sketching people and buildings. This penchant continued when he was a clerk at Henley's and, in 1919, when he heard that an American motion picture firm, Famous Players Lasky, was opening a London office, he applied for work as an artist, showing samples of his drawings he thought might be used for title cards. (During the era of silent filmmaking, elaborately drawn title cards provided dialog and held the plot together for the more unsophisticated filmgoer.) He was hired and thus his film career began.

For six years Hitchcock was a studio workhorse, willing to take on any kind of job. He was utterly fascinated by film and gave his life to it. (He was then, as he would be through most of his life, a strict abstainer from alcohol and tobacco but compensated by consuming great quantities of food which produced a permanently overweight, penguinesque body.) He slaved away at Famous Players Lasky as a designer, assistant director, and script writer. In 1922 he was to direct a film called *Number Thirteen* which was to star Clare Greet, the actress, who was financing her own film. When the money ran out, the production collapsed. Nothing remains of this first unfinished Hitchcock film.

Not until 1925 did Hitchcock again get the chance to direct. His superiors sent him to Germany where, working under the banner of UFA, the renowned German film com-

The 39 Steps, 1935: **Lucy Mannheim telling Robert Donat that the leader of the spy ring he is seeking is missing a finger (top).** *The Lady Vanishes,* 1938: **Dame May Whitty registering at a hotel before disappearing (bottom).**

pany, Hitchcock directed *The Pleasure Garden,* the story of
two chorus girls, one good and one evil. It met with critical
success and Hitchcock was put to work on his second film,
The Mountain Eagle, loosely based on some legendary Ken-
tucky feuds. This film was also a success and allowed Hitchcock to select his own project. He leapt at a suspense-thriller,
The Lodger, which was based upon Jack the Ripper. This
1926 film established Alfred Hitchcock as a master of the
dark genre he would later monopolize.

As with all of his succeeding films, *The Lodger* was indelibly marked by the Hitchcock touch, a story told at fast pace,
bold camera angles that startled, even frightened, the viewer
but worked in unison with a tale of terror, quick cuts and
closeups to further emphasize apprehension and fear on the
faces of his actors. And it was in *The Lodger* that Hitchcock
made his first personal appearance as a shadowy figure in a
busy office scene, a trademark employed in all the films he
directed thereafter. (Almost immediately following the success of his first suspense-thriller, Hitchcock married Alma
Reville, whom he had met some years earlier at Famous Players Lasky, where she was employed as a writer. The union
produced one child, Patricia, who later became an actress,
appearing in some of Hitchcock's films.

The director produced one great suspense film after another in England for ten years (1929-39) including *Blackmail,
Murder, The Man Who Knew Too Much* (this 1934 classic
remade in America in 1956), *The Thirty-nine Steps, Secret
Agent, Sabotage* and *The Lady Vanishes.* Moving to the
United States in 1939, Hitchcock's output continued to be
phenomenal and always matchless—*Rebecca, Foreign Correspondent, Suspicion, Saboteur, Shadow of a Doubt* (his
favorite film), *Lifeboat, Spellbound, Notorious* (his second-
favorite film), *Strangers on a Train, Dial M for Murder, Rear
Window, North by Northwest, Psycho, The Birds, Torn Curtain, Frenzy.*

There is no doubt in any film expert's mind that Hitchcock was an original, an innovator of the first class in motion

pictures. Filmgoers kept on the edges of their seats for 50 years also bear witness. Moreover, no director since Hitchcock's death (in his Bel Air, California home on April 29, 1980, after a year's illness), has managed to replace him as the master filmmaker of the suspense-thriller. He was, like his films, one of a kind, unique.

The following interview with Alfred Hitchcock took place at the Ambassador East Hotel in Chicago, December 1969, when his spy-suspense epic, *Topaz* was about to be released. (The interview appeared in *Chicagoland Magazine*, January 1970.) The author entered Hitchcock's suite while the director was on the phone talking long-distance to a friend and complaining about Deborah Kerr's role in a current film. "My Lord," Hitchcock was saying in that unforgettable raspy voice, "she takes *all* of her clothes off! Can you imagine her doing something like that?" As I sat down on a couch and waited for the director to finish his call I remembered Hitchcock's own film, *Psycho*, in which, ten years earlier, he had introduced, however tastefully and briefly, nudity to the American screen, presaging yet another trend.

Finishing his phone call, Hitchcock turned, walked to a chair and sat down quietly, studying the author from head to toe. He then stood up and put on his suitcoat before again taking his seat. A large serving table on wheels was piled high with empty breakfast dishes. Hitchcock peered into black coffee and orange juice waiting on the coffee table. "Is that me?" he asked an aide while pointing to the beverages. Then he folded his hands across his expanse and began to talk. His conversation, like his films, was witty, searching and thickly caked with his constant sense of macabre humor.

In your latest films The Birds, *and your most recent,* Topaz, *you seem to be practicing a taste for comparatively unknown actors. Is there a reason for this?*

I think that the simple fact is that there aren't enough stars to go around. Many of them form their own companies. And they only want to do pictures on their own and preferably they like to

hire a rather junior director so that the star can tell him what to do, what they want.

F. Scott Fitzgerald once stated that Ernest Hemingway required a new woman for each of his books, a new wife. Rarely have you employed the same star except James Stewart and Cary Grant to play your male leads. They are all different, as if you were testing, experimenting. Is this a cathartic trait of yours, like a novelist never being able to write of the same subject again?

No, I don't think, broadly speaking, that's actually correct because, after all, I did have Grace Kelly in many pictures.

I meant male leads.

Well, that would depend upon the story. You see, if I'm doing an adventure story, I think the story is helped by having a familiar figure in trouble because the audience will root much more for him than they will an unknown. If it's Cary Grant on the run and in danger, they'll worry about him like they would worry about a relative, but a lesser-known man, they might say—you know—poor devil. I liken it to the street accident where you see the man lying there and you say, poor devil. Take a second look and it's your brother and think of the change in the emotion.

With the exception of the suave Mr. Grant, almost all of your leading men, including James Stewart, are sort of the common man-next-door types. For the most part, they have, irrespective of their star status, plain and forgettable faces. Is this because all of them have always been victims?

That is definitely designed. That is to take average ordinary men and put them in bizarre situations.

Is this because they always seem to be victims?

Yes, surely.

The victim theme is, apparently, your favorite. How does this relate to you? Do you see yourself in the role of the victim?

Not necessarily, no, although I'm not what you might call an aggressive type.

You once told someone you were cowardly . . . a frightened man who bolted his door at night thinking a madman was on the other side waiting to slit your throat. Why do you feel this way about yourself? Is it because of the films you've made?

Saboteur, 1942: **Norman Lloyd threatens Priscilla Lane in the head of the Statue of Liberty, a scene cut from the film (top).** *Foreign Correspondent*, 1940: **Heavy Eduardo Ciannelli grilling a drugged diplomat, Albert Basserman (seated), held captive (bottom).**

That sounds a bit extreme but to be a little more psychological I can give you a quote about me by Ingrid Bergman, when she said of me: "That's the trouble with him. He won't ever have a fight."

You are both a constant student and a master of presenting evil. In Foreign Correspondent, Saboteur, North by Northwest, *and* Topaz, *evil is organized, a system. In other films such as* Spellbound, Strangers on a Train *and* Psycho, *evil is singular and the result of insanity lurking in one man's mind. You seem to waver between these two poles. Which do you feel the most important as far as audience impact goes?*

Well, I think that somebody once said the better the heavy, the better the story. The menace coming from an individual is a pretty strong thing. If you take the premise of *Strangers on a Train,* well you do have an insane man and a very dangerous one. He says if you kill my father, I'll kill your wife for you. And the other guy finds himself caught up with this evil, insane person. You're getting it today with this Tate case [Actress Sharon Tate, murdered by the Charles Manson "family"], where one man with a record gets a lot of hippies to go along with him.

You mean what is being claimed by some as mass hypnosis?

I don't think so. [Manson] manipulated these other people and with them it's a dare.

Probably the most frightening development of the madman character for me in your films was Robert Walker in Strangers on a Train. *Up to the time of that film, Walker had been known as a pretty boy, a nice guy. How did you get him to achieve the transformation to the role of the berserk killer?*

It was type casting.

In other words it came perfectly natural to him?

You bet your life. I remember one night we had him at a party, God rest his soul, he's dead now, a little party after the picture's showing at our house and my wife gave him brandy. Someone said—Oh, you should never do that, never give him brandy because he'll be gone. And he was gone, too. He had two or three. Then he took my wife aside and talked about me. He said, "You know I love him, but I hate him at the same time." This was Robert Walker. It's scary, isn't it? In our own home!

Your films are consistently stamped with a feeling of mobility —trains, cars, planes, boats—functional transportation that seems to hold terror almost in itself. Why this device? Do you fear travel?

No, I'm crazy about travel. As a kid my favorite reading, and it is to some extent today, was timetables. One of the best time-tables I used to enjoy and I still do—although it's a shadow of what it used to be—is Thomas Cook's Continental Timetable.

Sort of a Cook's tour?

Well it was rather a Cook's tour in that respect. You know I've taken many a ride on the Trans-Siberian railway. The strangest hobby I had as a little boy—when I was about 10 or 11—in respect to travel . . . I had a map of the world. It was about that big [spreading his arms to their full extent] I used to keep it in my room and I used to make tiny flags like the ones they used to mark the battle lines in World War I with. I used to paint on each flag the house flag of a shipping line . . .Cunard, P&O, White Star, and then the name of the ship printed on the flag. I used to buy Lloyds Daily Register of Shipping which gave all the movements of all the ships out of England all over the world and I would move these flags every two or three days. You know the one line I could never do? It was Cunard . . . or White Star [thinking]. Because once it left Bishop's Rock, which is at Land's End, England, you heard nothing from them and there was nowhere to put it un-til it hit Ambrose Light outside of New York harbor. Whereas if you were tracking a P&O line, which went to Australia, you knew. It went down the Channel, it passed Ushant, which is in Brittany, then it crossed the Bay of Biscay and hit Cape Finisterre, another important light. All the ships were marked by the lights and the messages were sent back. And then down the coast and through the straits of Gibraltar, up to Marseilles, and then down across to Port Said, down the Canal, past Aden, right at the tip of the Red Sea, into Bombay and from Bombay down to Colombo and then across to Perth, Australia. Six weeks it used to take to follow one ship.

And this was your hobby?

Hobby, yes. But not one ship—all the ships of the line—South

African ships, ships to Australia, India, and so forth. The most important lines.

Does this explain your penchant for the mobility device?

Yes, I was very interested in travel. To me, the most interesting—now this sounds like I'm talking like Robert Walker—like I'm nuts—to me the most dramatic moment is when the last rope drops from a departing ship. There's no more connection with the shore. The gangways are gone . . . .

That's kind of fatalistic.

Well, as I say, you could call me Robert Walker. Almost a similar thing was to stand by a locomotive there at the London Station . . . next to a long-distance train that you knew was going a helluva long way and see that thing stationed and suddenly it started. It wasn't the fact that it was just moving away, it was the imagination of where it was going. Point? The point wasn't that it was the moment of going, of departure: it was the knowledge that it was going a long way. Planes are dull, and so are trains today . . . uninteresting. The diesel locomotive is very dull compared with steam locomotives. There's no vitality . . . there's just a blah . . . .

Do you see these vehicles in themselves as holding some sort of mystery for your audience?

Yes. I didn't see them like Lubitsch did when he had Jeanette MacDonald singing "Beyond the Blue Horizon." She was having a love scene on the train and he cut to the piston going in and out.

You have made personal appearances in almost all your films. Do you do this as a traditional stamp or for luck?

No, it just became sort of a gag.

Psycho *was one of the first to employ, unlike most of your pictures, some very sexy scenes. Do you think this might have inadvertently triggered the upward surge in fleshy film making?*

I don't think so. No, I think that the "nudies," as they call them today, are merely an extension of the permissiveness of society as a whole. After all, don't forget that *Psycho* was made in 1960. That's nine years ago . . . although it's shown today, it still is current. I mean it's *lived* nine years . . . it's still living. *Psycho*, as a film, is still a living thing. It's talked about, it's shown and this, I think, is the most important thing about that picture . . . its longevity, where most films last a year . . . a year-and-a-half.

You feel this way about the majority of the films you've made?

Well, somehow, they do survive, I don't know why. For example, people look at a picture like *Notorious* on TV and they say, well, that could have been made today. I think it's the manner and style of telling. Content, you see, has never been of any interest to me, but the style and manner of telling the story . . . that's the thing that makes them last.

Do you think Foreign Correspondent *could have been made today?*

I think so, yes . . . as an adventure.

Where did you shoot Foreign Correspondent?

Part of it was shot in Holland, the chase, during wartime. It wasn't easy to get. I got an English cameraman to go over. He lost his first lot of gear when he was torpedoed and he had to go over a second time to shoot this chase of the cars through the Holland villages. Then we built the windmill on the set. Strangely enough, the heavy, Herbert Marshall . . . I really got that idea about him from Dr. Buchman of Moral Rearmament—you know—"peace, peace, and everybody love each other," and all the time he was an agent.

You took great pains of accuracy to recreate the façade of the Russian Embassy in Copenhagen for Topaz, *yet you shot* Lifeboat *almost completely in a studio tank. Was your drive for accuracy in* Topaz *important to you other than that of a political motivation?*

I think the important reason of the accuracy was the nature of the story being told in actual locales. *Lifeboat*—well, you couldn't have very well gone to sea to do that. You could never get the mobility of the shots. If I had gone off Santa Monica and shot it from a floating platform, you would have had this going on all the time [Hitchcock moved his hands rapidly, simulating waves]. I would have had no control over it. A film like that would have been impossible to shoot at sea. For example, all your angles. If I had gone out on a raft . . . let's say it was a calm sea and I was shooting into the boat there, I would have almost been down

Shadow of a Doubt, 1943: Killer Joseph Cotten, his niece Teresa Wright and banker Clarence Muse in Hitchcock's favorite film (top). *Lifeboat,* 1943: Stranded at sea with a maniac aboard are (left to right, top row) Walter Slezak, Mary Anderson, Hume Cronyn, Tallulah Bankhead, Henry Hull, Heather Angel, (bottom row) John Hodiak, William Bendix and Canada Lee; the film was shot completely in the studio tank, and Miss Bankhead proved difficult (bottom).

[duckbilling his hand and indicating a severe downward angle].
There would have been no way to get level with the people. As it
was, in order to get at the people in the boat, I had to have three
lifeboats—one full-length, a half of one, and a half of one split
down the middle—and we brought up whichever one was useful
for the shot. It wasn't just shot in one boat.

*Was Tallulah Bankhead temperamental with you in the shoot-
ing of* Lifeboat?

No, great. We got along wonderfully well. The only difficulty
was that the women on the set complained that she was climbing
in and out of the boat with nothing on underneath. So the union
manager came to me and said that "The women on the set are
complaining about Miss Bankhead—she's got nothing on! And they
want me to speak to her." I said, "Well, you know she's a fire-
brand—she'll tear you to pieces . . . and she probably hates your
guts anyway." And he said, "What am I to do? Will you tell her?"
I said, "Not me, first of all I'm on loan from Selznick and I don't
even work for 20th Century-Fox. You better go and see Zanuck
up front and ask him or Lou Shriver, his assistant." So he came
and said, "I've got to tell her." I said, "I wouldn't if I were you. I
don't think it's your department." He said, "Well whose department is it?" I said, "Either hair dressing or makeup."

You began your film career in London—

I'm actually American-trained. I learned script writing and all
the technical side of the business in an American studio in London.
It was really Paramount and it was called Famous Players Lasky.

*Was there ever a chance you might have stayed in the writing
area?*

No. As a matter of fact around the years 1922, 1923, 1924, I
used to write the script and when I finished writing the script I became the art director on the picture. I was doing drawings and
everything. One day a producer told me that the particular director I was working for didn't want me anymore. I was sort of fired.
I asked "Why?" He said, "Well, I don't know." Of course, years
after the producer told me it was jealousy, because I was getting
all the credit for the films and he was just directing. But he was an
exhibitor anyway. He didn't have that vast knowledge of the tech-

nical side. I was asked if I would care to direct a picture and I said it never occurred to me, and it hadn't. I had no plans or ideas like they do today—everybody wants to direct. I was very happy doing the scripts and art direction.

I gather you don't care for the stars today who do their own direction?

I don't care for them shooting a picture at all. To me the creative end is finished when the script is finished. I work closely with the writer. I can visualize the finished product completely.

How much of the script for a movie do you actually work on?

I work on it from the beginning with the writer. It's not so much that I'm doing the writing, like dialog and character, it's the fact that I'm bringing the writer into the direction of the picture. I'm making him aware of how we ought to do certain things, how it should be shot. It's not a question of my taking his script and interpreting it. If the writer goes to see the picture, he will see exactly upon the screen what we have decided upon ahead of time. Many writers turn in a script and when they look at the picture it's all different from what they wrote.

Have you ever thought of doing any of Ray Bradbury's books on film?

Ahhh, no. I haven't dabbled in the science fiction area at all. I did on TV, but never on full-length film.

It seems as if the Bradbury films that were done—Fahrenheit 451 *and* Illustrated Man *were anemic and that his most important and interesting property,* The Martian Chronicles *has never been filmed.*

No, *The Martian Chronicles* have been hawked around a long time—our studio had it [Universal]—but the cost was enormous. And you run a terrible risk with a thing like that today because you'll have Mariner 4 come down and say "There's definitely no life on Mars." Then where are you? I was having breakfast years ago with H. G. Wells on the Blue Train going down to the south of France and I was discussing with him about making *The War of the Worlds* into a movie. This was back about 1936 or 1937. "No," he said. "If that had to be made into a film, I'd have to re-write it and invent all new weapons because the weapons I put

Notorious, 1946: **Leopoldine Konstantin, Ingrid Bergman and Claude Rains—the subject was spies and slow poison; "I hit upon Uranium 235 in wine bottles,"(top).** *Strangers on a Train,* 1951: **Farley Granger listens to Robert Walker outline his plans for murder (bottom).**

into *The War of the Worlds* have all been used—poison gas and all the rest."

Close to science fiction—what do you think of the 007 movies, the Flint flics, the Matt Helm things . . . what do these films do for the standard of suspense in American film-making?

They don't. People look at those and are entertained purely objectively. I don't think those films involve an audience. If you take things like *Goldfinger* with the flying circus of girls—they did attempt to tie up Sean Connery to some atomic device, there was an attempt at suspense there—and examine it you'll find that the hero is not in danger at all for a great deal of the film. In fact, isn't it Goldfinger who says come along with me and I'll show you what I'm going to do? And the hero did nothing. He just sat smiling having a cup of coffee.

Like Flash Gordon.

Yes, the enjoyment to the public is the outrageous devices, but I don't think the public gets really involved.

Huntley Haverstock of Foreign Correspondent—*is he based even remotely on Edward R. Murrow?*

That was written by Ben Hecht, actually. He would have known. [Ben Hecht, who had been dead six years by the time of this interview, was one of the 14 writers who worked on *Foreign Correspondent* and received no film credit, although he was certainly Hitchcock's favorite screen writer.] The tragedy is that we don't have those pros today in our writing. That's what I miss more than anything else. Ben was a master. He was like a man playing four games of chess all at once. He'd run four scripts— Rose Hecht, his wife would be one, Charlie Lederer would be another and a woman called Czenzi Ormonde, who I had on *Strangers on a Train*. They'd all work on them and he'd polish them. I remember when we were doing the picture *Notorious*, the script was unfinished and he'd gone off it and I had Clifford Odets on it, which didn't work out. I said, "Ben, I've got this script, it's not finished." He said, "Just dummy it out for me." And that's what we did. I and a woman—Selznick's assistant—Barbara Keane, roughed out the scenes with the dialog and we gave it to Ben and it came back all polished up.

Psycho, 1960: **Janet Leigh, a runaway thief pondering her future at Bates motel; ". . . it's still living."**

Did he have anything to do with having Bob Benchley being in Foreign Correspondent?

My idea.   But did you ever hear stories about Ben Hecht's child? Jenny? She turned out to be a monster. I used to go up to his house in Nyack and at 16 months old, this child would not go to bed unless she were dressed for the street, hat on, everything. He was very proud and he said, "Oh, you should hear Jenny talk. Long words." And I said, "Such as what?" He said, "Do you know the other day, she said 'fascinating'?" So when I got to the house, Ben told her, "Say 'fascinating'." She went "Aaannn— innnaaiinng." And they were teaching her A. A. Milne's Christopher Robin and Ben asked her, where do they change the guard, and the child went, "Nnnyaaa—unnng—in—aaice." And finally, he said, "You know we're teaching her ballet now," and he said, "Jenny, do a *pas seul*." This little tot did this. She went across the room [Hitchcock got up quickly and walked across the room, standing next to a chair] over to here. And went . . . [Hitchcock briefly raised his right leg in mimicry of a dog visiting his favorite fireplug] .

But the funniest story about Ben's child concerned Rose Hecht. She used to take this child out in a baby buggy and to amuse the child wherever she went, she'd climb a tree. So the child kept saying, "Mama-uhh, mama-uhh." And if she didn't climb a tree, the child would scream blue murder. So she's down the street one day and there are no trees and the child kept saying, "Mama-uhh, mama-uhh." So Rose Hecht—she was in her fifties nearly, a small woman—had to try and shinny up a power line pole. Here she is shinnying up the thing and a garbage truck goes by and stops and the guy says, "Can I give you a hand, madam?" Oh, this child. Only Ben could have produced her.

Do you ever find yourself getting into jams—developing a situation until it is almost unbelievable, like the end of Huston's Across the Pacific?

You mean where the script takes you sometimes?

Right.

Oh yes. Ben Hecht and I were working on *Notorious* and we had to say, well, what are the Nazis up to down there? Ingrid

The Birds, **1963: Tippi Hedren and children fleeing, under attack in the most sinister film Hitchcock ever made.**

Bergman is sent by the FBI with Cary Grant alongside her, and, until I hit on Uranium 235 in wine bottles, God, we had armed camps down there, the Graf Spee crew, we had Nazis drilling—you've never seen such a "MacGuffin" [the word Hitchcock always employed to mean the device or excuse for causing all the mystery and suspense in his films], the most elaborate thing. I remember saying, "Well, what are they doing it for?" We couldn't find out so I said, "We had better forget the whole thing. Let's start again." I know in *North by Northwest* it didn't end on Mount Rushmore in one version. We got up into Siberia nearly with it, Ernie Lehman and I. I remember I had a sequence where the girl is kidnapped. They get here across the straits and they're going along a road in Siberia in an open car and a helicopter from the Alaskan side is chasing the car with a rope hanging from it and they were saying to the girl, "Grab the rope!" And she's rescued from the car but the heavies try to grab her back. I don't remember if we had a man on the end of it or what, but it was the most daring rescue you've ever seen. I remember one scene I wanted. I said, "Can't we work on it somehow? We ought to have a scene showing a vast plain of ice and two little black figures walking towards each other . . . enemies or something." I don't know what would have happened when they got together.

Didn't Von Stroheim use something like that in Greed?

Greed? He may have done that, I don't know. I also tried to work in—they are going along and there is a hole in the ice, and, suddenly, a hand comes out of the hole. You've got to go wild and then tone it down.

Where would the hand come from?

I don't know. That's what you have to work out afterwards. See. That's the hard work. Get the idea, which is a startling thing, then you got to say how you came by that. You shock 'em first and explain later. That's the power of technique.

Next to The Lodger, *which was based on Jack the Ripper, your murderers and killers are far from historical, like, say, Bonnie and Clyde. Does the fictional killer allow you more freedom?*

Oh, yes, and not only that but the fictional killer allows you to be more realistic.

How so?

Well, the conventions always were or they used to be that the villain was an unpleasant man. Now I made this film with Thornton Wilder where the killer, played by Joseph Cotten, is a murderer of rich widows. He murders about three or four. [The film *Shadow of a Doubt* was loosely based upon the real-life exploits of a coast-to-coast lady-killer, Earle Leonard Nelson.] This is against all convention of heavies, but it's based on truth because, you said to yourself, how else could he have ever gotten next to any of his victims without charm, without attractiveness? And yet when you look at it the other way—when you say, how can you have an attractive, charming murderer, well, he's got to be that way. It won't make sense otherwise. There's Haigh, the acid-bath murderer in London. He got his rich women. He shot them and he got their money or got their money turned over to him and then he put the bodies in tubs of sulphuric acid and dissolved them away. At the trial, there were constant references to sludge. You know what sludge is? That's half-decomposed flesh. Sludge, they call it. How was he caught? They found in one of the tubs . . . dentures, plastic that the acid wouldn't pit. Funny thing about this man Haigh—it was a very famous case—when he was ultimately arrested, it was very simple. The manageress of this London Hotel . . . it was called the Onslow Court Hotel—do you know London at all?

I've only been there once.

It was in Kensington where they have those Regency houses, you know, with the big columns on the front door. Well, this was a hotel like three of those houses put together. And it was the under-manageress who noticed that this man went up with one of the hotel guests—he was living there as well . . . had lived there for some time—and took her up and came back without her. It was as simple as that. She didn't care for him very much, the under-manageress. So she told somebody and they said, well if you feel that way about it, then why don't you go to the police? She went to the police and they looked him up. They found he had a record. That's all it took. And they investigated the whole case and when he was arrested he told the police that he drank his victim's blood, which was all baloney because all he was trying to show was that he was insane so's not to get hanged. And he said to another policeman, "What's it like at Broadmoor?" Well, that's the criminal lunatic asylum in England. He was finally tried and hanged. He was tried before Mr. Justice Humphries, one of those leathery-faced old English judges who had been prosecutor for years for the government.

Sort of a Henry Daniell?

Older than that. Wizened, you know. And when it came to the time of his retirement—his wife died and he didn't want to live in the big house outside of London—he sold all his furniture and packed all his things and put them into his limousine and went to his place of retirement. Where do you think the limousine pulled up? The Onslow Court Hotel. The judge went to the very hotel which was the scene of the crime! And in his biography one of his aides mentioned this fact to the judge, and, it says in the book, "The judge merely laughed sardonically."

On that, let me ask you something frivolous. Could you have ever filmed a musical?

Musicals are really not done by one director. You know the real big musicals, especially the old MGM ones, were shot in a lot of stages. All the director of the musical did was shoot the straight scenes. No, it wouldn't interest me. If it did, it would have to be what the public would expect of me—the first chorus girl gets shot by someone . . .

That's not so strange. Ben Hecht, at the time of his death, was working on a musical about the Chicago gangster, Deanie O'Bannion.

Was he? They're doing a film now which has a section of one of Ben's stories in it . . . *Gaily, Gaily* . . . the one where they tried to get the body out—he told me that whole story. He and [Charles] MacArthur conceived the idea of claiming a body of an electrocuted man—hanged man—and reviving him. They had everything. They had a tent, a hospital tent nearby and they got everything set up because they were going to make a helluva big story out of it. Everything was going great, except that they had forgotten to bribe one man—one undersheriff who wouldn't let the body

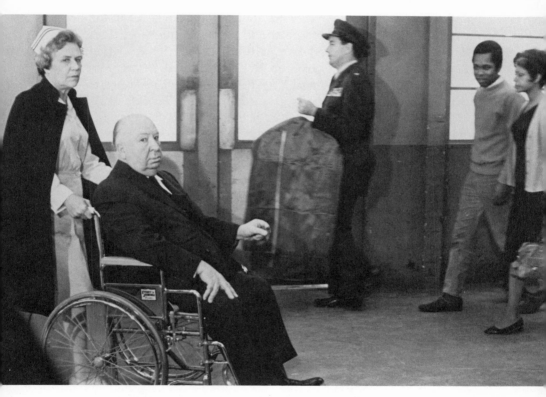

Topaz, 1969: Hitchcock appearing in his traditional cameo; "It was a gag."

go in time. Ben also told me an extraordinary story about how he was a witness at a hanging and he said he reported that a "black cat walked across the top of the gallows," and another reporter reported that "three black cats walked across the top of the gallows" and a third reporter said, "five." All different.

But the most fascinating story Ben told me was that he was in a courtroom and there were a lot of other reporters there and the defendant jumped up and went and stabbed the judge in the open court. All of them were petrified! They stopped writing. And Ben suddenly saw one reporter writing like anything, writing! And he called the boy and gave him the copy and as he went by, Ben said, "Well, Christ, I haven't written a thing, I'm going to grab this." He grabbed the copy from the boy and he looked at it and all it said was: "The judge has been stabbed, the judge has been stabbed, the judge has been stabbed, the judge has been stabbed, the judge has been stabbed . . . ." Isn't that a fascinating story?

Amazing.   You recently said that your latest film, Topaz, *is closer to* Notorious *than any of your other films.   Why?*

Only on the part of the adult nature of the espionage.

Is Notorious *your favorite film?*

One of them, yes.

William Faulkner once drew up a list of great contemporary writers of his own time—with Hemingway at the bottom, I might add.   Who would you place on such a list next to yourself of those who have created great suspense films?

I don't think anybody special.

Even foreign directors?

Well, you take Truffaut.   He's made a couple which are supposed to be what they call homage to me, but of course he makes other films.   He makes biographical films about his own life like *The 400 Blows.*

There was one unusual film by Billy Wilder, Witness for the Prosecution . . . .

Yes, well that was an isolated film, even for him.   That was a play.

You somehow manage to get your people off the hook at film's conclusion.   Yet in The Birds, *you seem to be saying that the winged creatures would eventually take over the world; still you allowed your stars to escape. Why?*

Because there was a situation where you had no reason at all to round it off. What are you going to do? Have all the birds fly away? It would seem to be a rather tame conclusion. If you looked at *The Birds* as a picture you might say, "What's it all about?" It's really that man, as we do, takes nature for granted, like birds, little dreaming that they can turn on you. They've been caged, shot at, eaten. Think what happens when man takes uranium out of the ground. Look what that's done.

Would you consider The Birds *as the most sinister film you've made?*

As an overall film, I would say so, yes.

One last question. If you were to be murdered, Mr. Hitchcock, which of the diabolic plans shown in any of your movies would you select?

To be murdered? Boy! [Eyebrows raised and then with a twinkle mellowing into a glint right at me] I think a nice overdose of arsenic would be as good as any . . . providing it wasn't too painful. You know, if you had a gun pointed at you, you would be inclined to say, "Be careful, that thing might go off!" And it does! Always reminded me of the story of the man being led to the gallows. He looks at the trap and he says, "I say, is that thing safe?"

Author Saul Bellow in 1944 at the time of his first published novel, *Dangling Man*.

Saul Bellow:
Light in Academe

Saul Bellow is a curious and aloof author, a Nobel Prize winner (1976) and holder of many literary awards, both domestic and foreign. He has been accused of being the "annointed author" of the academic world and, in some respects his work does correspond to the credos and quirks of the so-called New Criticism philosophy (as relating to levels of meaning, types of ambiguity and other assorted and ethereal gobbledygook). He is also, in spite of his totemic image, a superlative pathfinder in American literature, perhaps the closest thing we have to the Russian writers of the nineteenth century, particularly Turgenev, a master of the introspective narrative and the advocate of the hopeless hero.

The books that have been produced by Bellow—from *Dangling Man* to *Humboldt's Gift*—are of their own "school," separate and distinctive, apart from the mainstream and the notion of the popular; Bellow, of course loathes the popular as would any dedicated innovator, even though some of his books, such as the picaresque *Adventures of Augie March* and

Henderson the Rain King, have proved themselves immensely popular works.

As a public person, Saul Bellow hardly exists. He shuns publicity and rarely does he ever grant an interview, unless under extremely controlled circumstances. He is, like Mr. Sammler, reclusive, withdrawn, a literary hermit. The following interview, which took place in early June 1964 was forced upon him. The author, who at the time published and edited *Literary Times,* repeatedly called Bellow, and was put off time and again.

"I don't see any reason for it," he stated on the phone.

"Whatever time you can spare," I told him, "would be appreciated."

"Who'd want to read such an interview?" he asked, then added, "I have nothing to say." (It was later evident that Saul Bellow had plenty to say about his fellow writers, the state of American literature, the Nobel Prize and who deserved winning it, and chiefly and most importantly, his own work, about which he has scrupulously evaded comment through the years.)

The author finally prevailed upon Bellow to grant a brief interview, on his home ground at the University of Chicago, right in his back yard, inside his classroom. He would give me time between classes, and that was all. If the following interview, which appeared in the July 1964 edition of *Literary Times* appears a bit hurried and erratic in spots, it is. Bellow measured the questions and answers by the minutes, *constantly* looking at his watch throughout what for him must have been an ordeal.

At the appointed hour, the author positioned himself outside of Bellow's classroom door and, when the students filed out, I rushed in, taking a seat in the first row as Bellow stood behind a desk, wearing a wrinkled white shirt, slacks and a worried look. "This won't take too long," I told him, feeling like a dentist soothing a jittery patient unfamiliar with the contoured chair and the overhanging drills. It was a painless experience after all—for me.

Bellow at the time of *Herzog* and this interview, 1964.

What do you hear from Yellow Kid Weil?

Is he still alive? I haven't heard from him in years—since my article on him in *The Reporter* back in 'fifty-eight.

I think so. I hear he's in Argentina or some place.

Uh-huh.

Is it true that the galleys of your new novel were stolen from the post office here in Chicago and returned to you in tatters?

Yeah. Some crooks took it when they robbed the place. I hope the condition it was returned in doesn't constitute its first critical appraisal.

What's the title?

Herzog—H-E-R-Z-O-G.

What's it about?

[Shrugs.] How do I know?

How long is it?

About the size of *Henderson*.

Does it have the usual alienated "Bellow's" hero?

I didn't think they were alienated—I always thought the other guys were.

How about the typical "Bellow's" savior who acts on the hero?

Who saved anybody?

I'm thinking in terms of such characters as Kirby Allbee in The Victim, *Doctor Tomkin in* Seize The Day, *and King Dahful in* Henderson. *Characters who somehow made the hero see the light or who reconcile them to their fate.*

Well "savior" is the wrong word. I never intended anything so strong. But then, I'm a poor judge of my own work . . . most writers are.

What effect has the philosophy of Nietszche had on your work?

I haven't read him since school.

Incidentally, you attended the University of Chicago, didn't you?

Yes.

An English major?

No, anthropology.

The reason I asked you about Nietszche is that at least one critic (Marcus Klein) has noted a similarity between certain sections of Zarathustra *and the direction of action in* Henderson.

Not as far as I know.

F. Scott Fitzgerald, cruelly depicted in Hemingway's *A Moveable Feast*—**a depiction Bellow thought "was hilarious."**

Getting back to Yellow Kid Weil, you stated that he was a "masterful man who refused to be society's obedient slave."

Well, I thought he was a kind of artist, and conducted himself with wit.

Couldn't the same be said of Hitler and John Dillinger?

But they were brutal men. They had no wit. A man who kills another man in cold blood can never be a hero to me, especially a bloody tyrant.

In Distractions of a Fiction Writer, *you said that the modern author—the modern man—was threatened with "death by distraction." Could you comment?*

What I meant was that a great many distractions are presented to us and there are a certain group of people who exploit others in terms of these distractions. You know, the suburbs, two cars. Or in the novel, sex or violence.

Do you feel that these problems are greater for the novelist today than in the past?

Well, let us say with so many writers using gimmicks such as four-letter words and graphic descriptions of sexual scenes, it's harder to get the readers' attention. Since not only the so-called avant-garde and sick writers use this method, it makes it difficult for the serious writer.

Do you consider the present crop of novelists worthwhile?

Most of today's novelists are useless. They are strangely impressed with the futility of life.

Do you mean such popular authors as Harold Robbins?

[Nods a yes.]   They write for shock alone . . . exhibiting your genitals simply delights the middle class . . . it's everywhere . . . . Lennie Bruce and his kind provide this mood of fake emancipation and it's worth money.

What about the avant-garde today?

I don't think it exists. The reason being that you have to be able to have something to make a protest about to be in the avant-garde. All the great avant-garde movements in the past have been based on shocking the audience.

And this is no longer possible?

Right. We are reaping the harvest of nineteenth-century ideas

James T. Farrell; Bellow thought that if Farrell received the Nobel Award for Literature he would be "sublimely happy."

on sexual freedom. Whitman, Freud—(even the *Ladies Home Journal*, in recent years)—have been telling us that sex is okay.

In connection with the sexual license allowed the novelist today, Knopf and Gingrich [Alfred Knopf of Knopf Publishers, and Arnold Gingrich, then the publisher of *Esquire* magazine] *have been forecasting a school of puritanical novelists. Do you think this is likely?*

I think that people might again begin to find virtue interesting.

Do you chart your own novels according to plot or do they develop out of character?

I don't really know, but I guess more character.

Is it true that you modeled The Victim *on Dostoevski's* The Eternal Husband?

No!   The parallel is obvious now, but not then [when writing *The Victim*]. I was in a high state of excitement.

Would you consider yourself a full-time professional writer, even though you concentrate a great deal on the academic life in the way of teaching?

I don't think of myself as an academic person at all. As far as teaching here, I feel I'm only on loan to the University. [Bellow began teaching at the University of Chicago in 1963, a year before this interview was conducted, and is, at the time of this writing, in early 1982, still teaching at that school, an outstanding "loan" to say the least.]

Have you read Hemingway's posthumously-published A Moveable Feast?

Funny you should ask.   I've been reading it by sections just this week.

What was your impression of this work?

He seemed to have a revival of his talent. I enjoyed the section on Fitzgerald . . . it was hilarious.

But don't you think he exaggerated the entire incident with Fitzgerald, feeling him a keen competitor and realizing that this was one way to discredit him? [The reference was to Hemingway's story in which Fitzgerald asked Hemingway to evaluate the size of his penis and pronounce it satisfactory, the examination taking place in the men's room of a Paris bistro.]

Robert Frost—". . . didn't want to be a Bobby Burns."

Well, he always was unreliable in reporting . . . . I've also noticed that the underlying idea of his manliness was suspect . . . a curious weakness that betrayed his character.

Do you feel that John Steinbeck was deserving of his recent Nobel Prize?

It was regrettable. Steinbeck himself stated that he "didn't deserve it." What else can you say?

Do you feel that James T. Farrell, in view of his past 37 published novels and other extensive work in the field of letters, might deserve the Nobel Prize?

I earnestly hope he gets it. It would make Farrell sublimely happy and therefore he ought to have it.

What is your overall impression of James Baldwin and do you feel that he is aiding his race with his recent play Blues for Mister Charlie *so archly condemned by Claudia Cassidy and other theater critics?*

As a novelist I think very little of him. I rate his essays high and his novels low. His role in "the movement," if not tempered by people like Martin Luther King, could be very dangerous.

What reason would you give for his popularity?

What was the last thing?

Baldwin.

The American Negro has been abandoned and we have a great social evil to remedy.

Yes, but what reason would you give for his popularity? Do you believe that the public is buying him out of a stricken conscience?

Yes . . . out of liberal guilt.

Do you think he has aided his race?

Well, Baldwin is using issues . . .

What about you in Augie March?

I had no issues.

How do you feel about Ezra Pound's treatment by U.S. authorities during the immediate postwar period when he was confined as a "lunatic" in St. Elizabeth's mental hospital? Do you think this was a just act? [At the time there was a great deal of controversy surrounding the poet Ezra Pound, who had continued to live in

Ezra Pound, shortly before his death in 1972. "He's a fascist and a propagandist," said Bellow.

Italy during World War II and who had reportedly made propaganda broadcasts for the fascists, although he later claimed that he was compelled to do so in that his daughter was a virtual prisoner of the fascists and had he not made the broadcasts she might have been killed. Instead of being tried for treason, Pound was confined in a mental institution.]

I think he's a fascist and a propagandist, but he deserved a fair trial if he was insane.

Why do you feel that those whom he had aided so extensively into publication—Frost, Hemingway, Williams and others—waited so long (1958) before attempting to get him released?

I was for his release . . . I would have called for his release, but you see, nobody discussed the issue reasonably . . . . Frost told me once that Pound wanted to make a "Bobby Burns" out of him and he "didn't want to be a Bobby Burns" and so I think, in a way, he delighted in having old Ezra in there . . . .

There are predominantly several "schools" of writing today, according to many critics, whereby an author enters publication with a personal theme—a Catholic or Jewish theme. What would you consider to be the cause behind this?

I don't think they make themselves Jewish or Catholic writers. The critics measure or classify them that way.

Just one more question. The school of the enlightened homosexual is widely acclaimed today. What reason can you give for this?

This school has been constituted into a power group of its own, although I can't issue a blanket indictment . . . . People are curious . . . they want to see more and more of it . . . these repressed sexual tendencies . . . . [At this point, Bellow cut the interview off abruptly, as his next class was about to begin, and I was dismissed.]

Ernest Hemingway: The Young Years

The impact Ernest Hemingway (1899-1961) had on American letters is immeasurable, despite the rash of attacks on his work in recent years by academic snipers. Hemingway's literature was best protected by himself because when he was alive he could go on living it, a physical literature that, for some, required his breathing presence as verification.

As a stylist Hemingway could not be matched, although he was sometimes expertly imitated, a true innovator who discarded the form and syntax of the Establishment when he began to write in the early 1920s, and risked his own inventiveness against utter rejection by that very Establishment. This remained evident, from his first major work, *The Sun Also Rises* to *For Whom the Bell Tolls* and *The Old Man and The Sea* for which—ostensibly—he received the Nobel Award (1954), work that exemplifies man's risk as he struggles against a mutilating environment.

Unlike most of the writers of the nineteenth century, Hemingway drew upon his own experiences, in fact, set the style for the modern-day *roman à clef*, almost as if by design

he set forth to live each story he would later write. For him, without the experience, first-hand and hot with memory, there was no story to tell. He told an interviewer near the end of his life: "From things that have happened and from things as they exist and from all things that you know and all those you cannot know, you make something through your invention that is not a representation but a whole new thing truer than anything true and alive, and you make it alive, and if you make it well enough, you give it immortality."

The forming of Hemingway the writer began with Hemingway the youth, the boy from Oak Park, Illinois, where his first promising pieces of writing appeared in the local high school newspaper, a youth spent tranquilly in the Midwest, spent hunting and fishing in northern Michigan where his father owned a cottage at Walloon Lake. It was a life that went undisturbed, except for a brief period when Hemingway went off to write as a cub reporter for the Kansas City *Star*. Then came the war and with it an unforgettable traumatic experience, as an ambulance driver who became "the most wounded man of the war," an experience that engulfed Hemingway, changed him completely and almost overnight into an adult, into a writer. This transitional period, devastating as it was for Hemingway, molded the artist and made the legend.

These early years were profiled by the author, after extensive interviews with those who knew Hemingway at the time, in Oak Park and on the Italian front (the latter would provide the panoramic background for Hemingway's classic *A Farewell to Arms*). The profile was published in *Chicagoland Magazine* in August 1968.

Young boys all over America were dreaming of the Civil War in 1918. The real war that year had no specific name—distant, faceless, it evoked visions of America's old, genteel wars where rattling sabres echoed, troops huzzahed a brave, personal enemy, and young maidens in white wore roses in their hair while waiting for the trains from the silent fronts. But war in 1918 was wholly new, in

Ernest Hemingway as a teenager at Walloon Lake, Michigan.

Ernest's paternal grandparents (seated), Anson and Adelaide Hemingway, their children (second row), Nettie, Alfred, Clarence (Hemingway's father), George and Grace. (Historical Society of Oak Park)

Hemingway's birthplace (born July 31, 1899), 399 N. Oak Park Avenue, Oak Park, Illinois (top). The house where Ernest Hemingway grew up, 600 N. Kenilworth Avenue, Oak Park (bottom).

all dimensions divorced from gentlemen soldiers and wars of the past. It was big business and those fighting and dying inside of it had no identity in the conflict—except for a pocket area containing volunteers who found a different way to serve: The Red Cross Ambulance Corps.

William D. Horne, Jr., a young businessman and graduate of Princeton, 1913, in his early 20s, had been turned down by all the services because of bad eyesight. He could not go to the Great Adventure in Europe. While living in Yonkers, one day in early May 1918, he went to see a Colonel Utasi in New York City.

"I want to go to France as an ambulance driver," he told the colonel.

"Will you just as soon be an ambulance driver in Italy?"

Horne thought a moment. "Hell, yes." He had found his way.

In Chicago, about the same time, an 18-year-old scion of a famous business family, Frederick Spiegel, who had a bad right hand and had also been turned down by the Army, Navy and Marines, saw a small notice in the old Chicago *Post* asking for volunteers to drive ambulances in Italy. He ran down to a small recruiting headquarters, with a signed letter from his father, and enlisted in the little band headed for Italy. He, too, had found his way.

Out where the plains roll flat in Kansas City, two reporters were writing their daily copy, two young men—one, Ted Brumback, already a veteran of the Field Service experience in France in 1917 with bad eyes; the other an 18-year-old cub reporter from the sleepy town of Oak Park, Illinois, Ernest Miller Hemingway, also with bad vision—saw the notice requesting volunteers for the Red Cross Ambulance Service destined for the pages of their newspaper, the Kansas City *Star*. They didn't wait for the notice to appear, but enlisted immediately. They headed for New York, after a brief fishing sojourn in Michigan.

In the bustling, war-fevered New York, the young volunteers were billeted in cheap hotels, drilling and exercising on the roof of the Red Cross Building on the lower west side of New York. Italy was a long way off and the volunteers had no idea what awaited there.

Horne lucidly recalled that "What happened was that the Ital—

Hemingway, age 16, in Michigan with Paul Haase (top left). Hemingway (with cap, standing behind unidentified boy) in Michigan train station (top right). Hemingway (second from right) with (left to right) Morris Musselman, Lewis Clarahan and Procter Gilbert (bottom). (All from The Historical Society of Oak Park)

ians had taken a helluva licking in the fall of 1917 and they were damned near knocked out of the war and it was just by an act of God that they managed to hold these Germans from coming through way beyond Caporetto across the Po River. So, during that winter—the winter came down and nobody could fight in those mountains in the winter—it was perfectly obvious that in the spring the Germans would try to come on through and cut the line of the Po and put Italy out of the war. So, I presume, the powers that be decided that they would put some Americans, some American assemblance of power, on the Italian Front. So they enlisted 150 mental, moral and physically disabled characters like Ernie and me to drive ambulances—on the Italian Front . . ."

These 150 Americans, including other Chicagoans Jerome Flaherty and Laurie Barnett, hoped they would be placed in Section IV in Italy as drivers. "It was the best, the cream," Horne remembers. "That section was up high in the mountains."

"I actually put in for Section IV," Spiegel says, "because that was a Fiat [Fiat ambulances were used in this sector of the Italian Front] and I had no idea of how to drive a Ford."

The volunteers sailed to Italy on the old USS *Chicago* from New York, heading first for Le Havre, France. They sailed for ten days on a churning sea, talked, shot craps, played poker, grew restless. Spiegel and Hemingway shared a compartment and Spiegel recalled the young Hemingway as "taking notes" on the voyage over.

"And there was a crap game going over," Horne remembers. "Ernie was in that. You know, for nickels and dimes and an occasional quarter." Ernie was in it all right. According to Spiegel, he and Hemingway ran this realistically floating crap game in their own compartment for a while.

There was much to think of in those ten days, ploughing through the Atlantic, for the young Hemingway.

Back there on the Edwardian continent of America, wrapped in social teas on Sunday, proper decorum in the home, cupolas, white wooden verandas, parlor music, solariums filled with massive plants and pianos, lace curtains, knickers, high-button shoes, was Ernest Hemingway's innocent youth.

Oak Park, Illinois, at the turn of this century was a village town where professional editors, writers and businessmen took refuge from the roar of Chicago, its raw-boned big brother to the east. Its shady streets and stately homes represented the bastion of the middle class on top of its pole, peering sleepily over the land, enjoying long years of comfort and tranquillity.

It was into this world that Ernest Hemingway was born. His father was a well-to-do doctor, with a lucrative list of patients. His mother was socially active and a product of the Victorian Age, where parlor decorum was not a gesture but a mandatory ritual.

Edith Striker, Hemingway's teacher in seventh grade at Oliver Wendell Holmes School, only remembered him as "very likable and handsome." And she remembered an incident with Mrs. Hemingway. "Hemingway's mother came to school one day," she says, "and put her arm around me and said, 'You know we love you' but had a serious complaint. She said, 'I don't think you should be reading Jack London's *Call of the Wild*. It's not the kind of book young people should be reading . . . .' I went to my desk and withdrew the University of Chicago list of recommended books for reading at the seventh-grade level and showed Mrs. Hemingway that the book was listed. It did not change her opinion."

Hemingway's childhood was complacent and, perhaps, too crowded with the feminine world of his sisters, but there were those early trips with the family up to the cottage at Walloon Lake near Horton's Bay in Michigan where his father, an expert fisherman and hunter, taught him his deep love of the wilderness. The simplicity of life up in Michigan, the peace of the woodlands, was to remain with Hemingway to his death as an area of solace.

The Hemingway family that resided on Kenilworth Avenue in Oak Park was well known. Uncle George Hemingway sold vast tracts of real estate in the small town. Dr. Willoughby Hemingway had pioneered his name into the ranks of missionaries as the famous doctor who went to China and halted the bubonic plague in a province there.

It was quite natural for Hemingway to attend the liberal arts-oriented Oak Park High School where his curriculum seemed to center in literature. Though many biographers, notably Charles

William D. Horne, who went to Italy with Hemingway: "There was a crap game and Ernie was in that," (top left). Hemingway in Paris after leaving Oak Park, Illinois, for good (top right). Frederick W. Spiegel, Jr., who served in Italy during World War I with Hemingway: "We were mostly kids, eighteen, nineteen . . . " (bottom left). John Gehlmann, Hemingway's English teacher at Oak Park High—"Ernest got me in trouble," (bottom right).

Fenton and Carlos Baker, credit two teachers there, Fannie Biggs and Margaret Dixon, with encouraging young Hemingway to write, a classmate and subsequent writer, Robert St. John, wrote, "Ernest and I had the identical experience with one particular teacher who told us we could never become writers. Ernest, at that time, decided to become a famous doctor like his father."

This particular teacher remained nameless, but it is true that Miss Dixon and Miss Biggs provided an active interest for Hemingway in literature. In 1913, Hemingway was in Frank Platt's freshman English class where he consumed everything from H. A. Guerber's *Myths of Greece and Rome* to *Ivanhoe*. Outside of class, Hemingway devoured the works of H. G. Wells.

On Sundays, the Hemingways sat together in church and heard the sermons of Dr. William E. Barton, who had written several books on Lincoln.

Summers were lazy and deep for Hemingway and, with the family or alone on a run-away, he inevitably returned to Northern Michigan. A classmate, Lewis Clarahan, remembered that "we took a trip to Walloon Lake. We hiked overland. All the way, Ernest would be making up things, talking at the top of his voice to the trees, just letting his imagination run wild. He had a typewriter on the third floor of his home in Oak Park. He took me up there once and was very enthusiastic in showing me what he had written."

And write he did, at every possible turn, including work for the Oak Park High School magazine, *Tabula*, for which he wrote his novice stories, "Judgement of Manitou" and "A Matter of Color." He also wrote satire and reports for the school's newspaper, *The Trapeze*, mostly in the manner of his idol of the day, Ring Lardner.

English teacher John Gehlmann arrived at Oak Park High School in Hemingway's senior year and was assigned to oversee the school newspaper. "I remember Ernie all right," Gehlmann says, "he got me in trouble every week. Ernie was the athletic editor of the *Trapeze*—which was normal, since he had been on the football and swimming teams—and at that time he was writing an imitation of Ring Lardner. Lardner had made a reputation for himself by writing up baseball news in baseball slang. Of course, certain faculty members thought it was horrifying for material of this nature to appear in the *Trapeze*. So, every week I was up on the carpet to explain how this sort of thing was allowed in the *Trapeze*. At any rate, I gave Ernie his head and took the weekly criticism. There were statements made that if I had not done this, Hemingway would have been downed with frustration and criticism as a writer. But that is not true. Nothing could have stopped Ernest Hemingway. He was on his way."

In 1918 he was on his way to Italy, to Red Cross Ambulance unit, Section IV, located at the railhead, Schio. He, along with Spiegel, Horne, Barnett, Flaherty, Art Meyers, and dozens more were made honorary lieutenants and given officer's uniforms. They wore stars on their sleeves and Red Cross emblems on their high collars—Sam Browne belts, gloves and those highly-polished riding boots.

This elegantly attired group landed at Le Havre and went up to Paris to await their train for Milan, Italy. Hemingway's first and only night in Paris during the war was "delirious with excitement," according to Ted Brumback. And, according to Spiegel, "Somebody had won all the money in the crap game, I forget who, and he decided to treat us all to a night on the town. He took us to a French restaurant—I had only been in Paris once when I was 12 years old—but we went to this particular restaurant and ate ourselves sick, and the next morning all of us awakened with the damndest case of hives you can imagine because we had been eating this bland food on the boat for ten days and then we went to this French restaurant with fancy food, wine and alcohol of all kinds. The next morning we were blotched all over . . . ."

Brumback told the story that during that brief stay in Paris, Hemingway and he took a taxi in a wild ride around the town, following the shell bursts caused by Big Bertha in the first German shelling of Paris. "We'll get a story for the *Star*," Hemingway said during the ride, "that'll make their eyes pop out in Kansas City!" They spent over an hour with their heavily-tipped taxi driver, trying to catch up with the bursts. Finally, they met the war. They saw "the shell hit the façade of the Madeleine," Brumback remembered, "chipping off a foot or so of stone. No one was hurt. We heard the projectile rush overhead. It sounded as if it were going to land right in the taxi with us. It was quite exciting."

"There was a Captain Somebody in charge of us," Spiegel said. "And we were supposed to obey his orders, but you can imagine a bunch of kids doing that. We were mostly kids, 18, 19, some older fellows like Bill Horne who was in his 20s and some as old as 45, like Yakima Harris, who came from Yakima, Washington."

Ernest Hemingway found it hard to wait to catch up with the war. "He was about the most exuberant young man I've ever met," Horne said. "He was a spectacular extrovert. He was looking for new experiences all the time."

After four days in Milan, Hemingway got his chance at experience at the town of Schio, north of Vicenza. Horne remembered: "We all thought we were the lucky ones—there was Percy Norton, my roommate at college, Hemingway, Spiegel, Barnett, Flaherty, Brummy [Brumback], Zalmy Simmons [heir to the Simmons mattress company], and half a dozen other guys—all were sent to Section IV. That was a beautiful section. It was stationed at the foot of the Dolomite Mountains and the Dolomites rose from the Venetian plain like the walls of a room. This was about two or three miles north of Schio. We were on the end of the line that pivoted on neutral Switzerland."

This was a peaceful front, except that one morning Hemingway and his compatriots woke up—wondering why they had been awakened at four o'clock in the morning—"and we heard these awful sounds coming in," Horne said, "they were bigger shells than 75s; they were 160s at least, great big ones—high-trajectory fire coming over from the Austrians about 15 miles away. They were trying to break up our railhead there at Schio. We were under bombardment there for some hours."

Hemingway was jubilant. "Oh, Boy!!!" he wrote home. "I'm glad I'm in it."

During the bombardment, Brumback and Hemingway set off at a run for the railway station where the bombs were falling, but, again, as in Paris, the bombardment ceased without too much damage and the war faded that day.

Life at Schio for the Midwesterners settled into a regular, monotonous routine. Bill Horne: "We never personally saw much trouble after that bombardment at Schio except that we'd drive up into the mountains where our posts were and pick up the wounded. We had three or four different posts to which one or two cars had to go and we went every day to pick up the wounded. That was the front. It was 10, 15 miles away at the most. We'd drive up to our posts. It would be called the advanced dressing posts. And they would load up our car and then we would drive it back to the Smithstemento and the Smithstemento was a hospital clearing house and they would mark each paper for each hospital which would receive each wounded man. We would sort of take them and retail them."

There were two Americans to each big Fiat truck. Horne was with Carleton Shaw. Spiegel was with Brumback, but only for a while. "Oh, he was terrible," Spiegel recalls. "He kept jerking the truck around those awful roads. On and off the accelerator. We parted company and I drove alone after that."

Each day the drivers would grind their trucks up to the front and return to base hospitals with their loads of bleeding men, and it was in the warm river of this routine that Ernest Hemingway learned so much of human life, of human death, slow, mutilated life ebbing into death back there in the rear of his big Fiat, all of it pooling and welling years later in that infinitely tragic book, *A Farewell to Arms*.

And before that majestic book of love and death in the pure, high Alps, Hemingway was writing on his cot in the Red Cross quarters at Schio. "Yes," Bill Horne asserted. "He was writing even then. Even then the spark of genius was in him."

The group of volunteers swam in a nearby stream when not on duty. "Oh, a dead chicken or something dead would float by once in a while," Frederick Spiegel remembered, "but no one thought much of it. We were at war." But the war went slowly at Schio for Hemingway. It got dull and Hemingway longed for the real war that constantly seemed to fade from him, retreating always to another sector.

Bill Horne: "Because there was nothing doing at Schio and

A rare photo shows Ernest Hemingway wearing an American officer's uniform and an Italian helmet at Fassalta de Piave, about July 1-8, 1918, shortly before being wounded in a front-line listening post. (Courtesy of Carlos Baker) there was some action down on the Piave—the Austrians hadn't quit yet on the Piave—they called for volunteers from these various drivers' sections to go down to the Piave and run canteens. You know, hand out cigarettes and candy. Hemingway and I and several others from our section volunteered for that service and we were driven down to the Piave River. They dropped me off at a town called San Pedro Novello with the 70th Brigade and they took Hemingway on to the next station which was called Fossalta —high moat, or whatever that means—and he was down there and nothing happened on that front. But he was very active. He went and got his chocolate and his cigarettes—he wasn't content with opening a little canteen somewhere. He got on this bike and rode around and went to the front line to a listening post and it was while he was in that they [the Austrians] dropped a *minewerfer* [a large mortar shell used by the Austrians] on him. It exploded and it killed a couple of guys. It wounded one man very badly. [In "Now I Lay Me" Hemingway recounts this momentous experience.] He dug this guy out [the man had no legs and Hemingway had been hit with hundreds of infinitesimal steel fragments from the explosion, one piece, according to Spiegel, working itself to the surface of his hand while the two sat in The National Cafe in Havana as late as 1958]. He dug the man out and got him on his shoulders and got him out of this wrecked listening post and started back to the Italian line. And the Austrians turned the searchlights on him and they turned the machine guns on him and he was stopped with a slug in the knee, a slug as big as the end of my thumb . . . but he got this guy back in. And then they invalided him. The first-aid guys sent him back to the field dressing post, and, fortunately, some other Red Cross driver, some ambulance guy found him there and then he began getting the good treatment."

It was at this precise moment, bloodied and hurt in front of his home lines with alien searchlights picking him out of the darkness there in Italy in 1918 and machine guns shooting him, the boy who had, moments before, been handing out chocolates and sneaking a look at the Big War over the parapet, it was then that Ernest Hemingway became the casualty of the 20th-century

The proclamation put out by the town of Schio, July 4, 1918, calling on residents to display American flags and shout loudly in honor of the American Independence Day.

COMUNE DI SCHIO

Cittadini !

Ricorre oggi la FESTA NAZIONALE del grande POPOLO NORD = AMERICANO.

In ogni più remoto angolo della Penisola, il pensiero ed il cuore di ogni Italiano, che nel libero Paese degli STATI UNITI trova una seconda Patria, si volge in questo giorno al Grande Popolo che, il più puro idealismo, ha fatto entrare nell'immane conflitto, e che alla causa della LIBERTA' ha consacrato ogni forza, ogni risorsa ed ogni energia sì morale che materiale.

Cittadini !

Esponete le vostre bandiere e numerosi accorrete alle ore 20 nella Piazza Alessandro Rossi, dove durante un programma svolto dalla distinta Banda Militare, gli alunni ed alunne delle nostre Scuole Elementari, in onore della Grande Nazione, canteranno l'INNO AMERICANO.

Cittadini !

Consci del possente contributo che il glorioso Popolo Americano apporta al trionfo delle libere Nazioni, memori sempre che alla pia e nobile avanguardia della Croce Rossa, fanno seguito e scendono dalle Alpi in questi giorni le valorose baionette Americane pronte ad entrare in linea a lato degli eroici e fieri nostri combattenti, alto, sponta= neo, sentito erompa dai nostri petti il grido :

W IL GRANDE POPOLO NORD - AMERICANO

Schio, 4 Luglio 1918

Il Sindaco
BELTRAME - POME'

Stab. Tip. G. Menin & C. - Schio

world, receiving a wound so deep it would never really heal, never to be forgotten because the words in all his books and stories would keep it fresh and painful and memorable. He no longer had to chase the glory and honor of war. It found him—a year out of Oak Park High School and its lazy drama—alone, without trumpets and banners. Like Crane's Henry Flemming, in *The Red Badge of Courage*, he had come to touch the Great Death but it had touched him indifferently with cool malice and lamed him, exploding the revelation of vulnerability, of the kind of mortality Oak Park High School could not teach. It was July 8, 1918.

Hemingway was sent back to Milan where the larger chunks of metal were removed from his body. Horne, too, sick with a stomach disease, went to the hospital in Milan where he witnessed the love affair between Hemingway and an American nurse, Agnes von Kerosky, later immortalized as Catherine Barkley in *A Farewell to Arms*. Hemingway was in Milan until 1919, having come down with jaundice after months of recuperating from his wound.

"Ernest never threw off on his experiences in the First World War," said Bill Horne. "That was a strictly Hemingway phrase. To 'throw off on' is to deprecate . . . . His experiences in the First World War were vital. They were fundamental in his whole after-life. He never belittled his experiences in Italy as an ambulance driver and as a wounded man. That experience he had when he was 19 years old was probably the most important formative experience of his life . . . except his love affair with Ag'.

"We came back just after the Armistice was signed," Horne stated. "Hemingway came home sometime after Christmas. It was January. He was still in hospital and was undergoing therapy . . . baths and bicycle exercises [related in Hemingway's stories "A Way You'll Never Be" and "A Very Short Story"].

He was still in love with the American nurse but she had thrown him over for an Italian officer. Spiegel, Flaherty, and Barnett all came home to Chicago with medals.

Hemingway was met at the boat by Horne in New York. The city papers there blared: "Most Wounded Man of the War Returns" in banner heads. Horne brought a girl with him, his date. "Hemingway came off the boat wearing his full-dress uniform and an

A rare photo showing Ernest Hemingway (arrow) hanging from the side of an armored car in Schio, Italy during World War I (top). The ruins of Hemingway's armored car after being blown up. He was not driving at the time (bottom).

Italian cape with purple lining, limping. He was about the most romantic guy you could imagine. The three of us had dinner at the Plaza that night. And the girl was completely fascinated with Ernie. She never said a word to me all night."

Later that year, after Horne had gotten a selling job in Chicago, he heard that Hemingway was living up in Michigan at Horton's Bay. "He was chopping wood up there . . . doing day labor. He was terribly hard hit by that Ag' situation, the collapse of that love affair with that nurse in Milan. He was terribly hard hit and he was just a kid and that was the first time he had ever been in love. She was a bit older than he was . . . . Anyhow, he was up there in Michigan and was going to be a woodchopper all the rest of his life. He had been writing and I knew he liked to write and wanted to write and I had this wonderful job that paid me $300 a month and I also had $800-$900 cash that I had saved up . . . . I was the richest guy in the United States, so I wired him, 'Come on down, I've got a job and I'll grubstake you. Come down and you can write and I'll sell axles for the Standard Parts Company and this is a wonderful city and everything is jake.' So, damned if he didn't!"

Horne and Hemingway rented a 4th-floor walk-up room at 1030 North State Street and settled into life in Chicago during the toddling Twenties. After a short residence there, the two ex-ambulance drivers moved into Y. K. Smith's rambling Victorian house, joined by advertising-executive-to-be, "Dirty" Don Wright. The nickname for Wright was Hemingway's. "It was deliberate," Horne says. "At that time, he and 'Dirty' Don were very good friends. 'Dirty' Don at that time was presumably writing the great American novel, but he wasn't doing anything of the kind."

It was while at Y. K. Smith's house as a boarder, that Hemingway was visited by the established writer, Sherwood Anderson. "Sherwood was a helluva nice guy," Horne remembers. "Even before Hemmy and I moved over to Y. K. Smith's we visited there and Sherwood was there and we would have an evening where we would sit around and talk high-mindedly about literature and art. Sherwood, after reading Hemingway's stories, was very impressed by this new, young kid just coming along as a writer. Hemingway

Hemingway in the early 1920s, skiing at Gstaad, Switzerland.

took his criticism very well. Sherwood was a god. He had written *Winesburg, Ohio* and *Windy McPherson's Son*. He was enormous! Ernie was unpublished, he was only editing a magazine."

Hemingway's editing job for the *Cooperative Commonwealth* magazine was less than inspiring. He wrote and edited human-interest stories for the periodical, owned by a highbinder named Harrison Parker, who later came under investigation for his manipulation of his farmer's cooperative organization. It was "a pot-boiling job," according to Hemingway's own description. "But it kept him alive," Horne added.

The budding writer and Horne ate most of their meals at Kizo's, a Greek restaurant at State and Division streets (the same Division Street later immortalized by Studs Turkel). "We got soup, steak, green peas and apple pie for sixty-five cents," Horne recalled with a smile, also remembering that he paid for all the meals until Hemingway got on his feet, and began running the *Cooperative Commonwealth*. "He paid me back," nodded Horne, "but I wish to hell I had never taken the money."

When Hemingway learned that Parker was bilking his readers in mail-order schemes he quit his job and wrote an expose of the magazine and his employer. He attempted to sell the story to every newspaper in the city but he was universally rejected. "Who was Ernest Hemingway, compared with Harrison Parker," snorted Horne. "He was a great God-gifted reporter. His material which had appeared [earlier] in the Kansas City *Star* and the Toronto *Star* was some of the greatest journalism ever written. Why some city editor could not recognize this genius and hire him is beyond the imagination."

This was also a period when Hemingway became absorbed with boxing; he and Horne spent a great deal of time working out in Kid Howard's gym. The two even sparred in Y. K. Smith's apartment, and, on one occasion, Horne dropped his guard for a moment and Hemingway landed a right cross that staggered him. "I was out standing up," Horne remembered with a grim smile.

In the fall of 1920, Hemingway met his first wife Hadley Richardson at a party held by Y. K. Smith. Horne witnessed the meeting: "Ernie and Hadley fell in love and it was like falling off a

Hemingway at the zenith of his literary career in the late 1950s.

pier. It was terrific! They got engaged and then we all went up to help them get married at Horton's Bay."

The Hemingways moved back to Chicago where, for a few months, the writer doggedly haunted the newspapers but was refused employment. He was contacted by the Toronto *Star* for which he had written several articles dealing with the war. He was hired as a foreign correspondent and was sent back to Europe, to Paris (at about $35 a week).

When Hemingway left Chicago, he was never to return, except on "passing-through" visits. There were other wars waiting; literary lions like Scott Fitzgerald, Ford Madox Ford, Gertrude Stein, James Joyce roaring through the streets of Paris in the days of the expatriates, were to become Hemingway's friends; *The Sun Also Rises* was to be written there, and the years held out the mysteries of Africa, the agony of Spain, another world war, Cuba and then Idaho, where the writer was buried after his death in 1961.

The Chicago ambulance drivers kept in contact, phoning Hemingway in Cuba and in Idaho with their wives when holding a reunion and visiting with him in Havana in the Fifties. In the end, Bill Horne, the man who went after the first great adventure with Hemingway those long years ago in Italy, bore him to the grave as a pallbearer on the silent, open plain in Idaho.

Hemingway wrote little of his hometown, but in 1952, he stated, "I had a wonderful novel to write about Oak Park, and would never do it because I did not want to hurt living people."

Karsh and the Faces
Of History

The greatest portrait photographer in the world is a traveling man. He is Yousuf Karsh. He flits about the globe in every conceivable kind of aircraft, seeking to photograph the most memorable people of our time.

At the turn of the century, the American crown of fashion and personal distinction was worn by those who had their portraits painted by the illustrious John Singer Sargent. If John Singer Sargent had brushed your image onto his canvas, you possessed a kind of immortality, a position, a rank, a station in life from which you could never descend. You became history itself.

The John Singer Sargent of today is Yousuf Karsh, a small, quiet man of extreme emotional sensitivity. Karsh has the uncanny ability to capture the world's most memorable faces at the zenith of emotion. Kings, presidents, popes, artists, tycoons, Nobel Prize Winners, boxers, and field marshals have stared, glared, mused, and posed before his camera's eye.

In the end, we are left with a texture, a beauty of composition, mood, simplicity, and absolute genuineness in Karsh's photos unlike anything else that has been achieved with a camera since Matthew Brady recorded the poignant history of the American Civil War.

Photography has not come to an end with Yousuf Karsh, which this modest, kind man would be first to admit, but it has developed to a fine art through his creations and those of his peers.

Karsh portraits have appeared in publications throughout the world, dominating such graphic powerhouses as *Life*. His work is represented in permanent collections at the Museum of Modern Art, the Metropolitan Museum of Art in New York, and the Art Institute of Chicago, to name a few. Many of the famous faces photographed by Karsh have appeared in *Faces of Destiny, Portraits of Greatness, Karsh Portfolio* and *Karsh Portraits*. His autobiography, *In Search of Greatness*, appeared in 1962.

Photos taken by Karsh since he embarked upon his distinguished career as a portrait photographer in 1932 have included British King George VI and Princess (later Queen) Elizabeth, Winston Churchill (his first truly great portrait), which later appeared on the stamps of six nations, U.S. Presidents John F. Kennedy and Lyndon Johnson. World-renowned artists, from Pablo Picasso to Pablo Casals, from Ernest Hemingway to Jean Julius Sibelius, have been captured by his camera. If one can think of a great composer, a master painter or writer, a stellar humanitarian, scientist, religious leader, then one can easily assume that Yousuf Karsh has taken their portraits, and etched their faces upon the memory of the world.

Much has been said of Karsh's techniques, that he has "darkroom secrets" by which he achieves his amazing photos, wholly unlike any taken by other photographers. His "secret" has nothing to do with his photographic equipment or careful processing; it is the man himself. "To make enduring photographs," Karsh once stated, "one must learn to see with one's mind's eye, for the heart and the mind are the true lens of the camera."

A Canadian citizen, Karsh lives with his wife, Estrellita, in Ottawa. His beautiful countryside home, Little Wings, is a bird sanctuary for multitudes of winged species. There are no photos, other than one portrait of Karsh's first wife, Solange, to be found at Little Wings. "I live with photographs all day," Karsh stated, "and so I do not have them at home; not even those of my family and friends."

The following interview took place at Chicago's Ambassador East Hotel in September 1967 and appeared in *Chicagoland Magazine*, October 1967.

You were born in Mardin in Asiatic Turkey in 1908?
I was born in Mardin in *Armenia-in-Turkey,* yes.
Can you tell me what your early life there as a boy was like?
Mardin has often been called the Garden of Eden, where man began. My father was a Catholic and my mother a Protestant. We suffered much at the hands of the Turks. Two uncles were killed by them. One uncle was suffocated to death after being placed in a cupboard. Another uncle was thrown alive into a well. The horror and the persecution of that time will remain with me all my life. This, of course, was the old Turkey of the First World War.
Did you personally experience any element of this terror?
As a boy, an Armenian Catholic, going to school, I was sometimes stoned by Turkish boys. One day, I placed many stones in my pocket. I intended to fight back. And I did retaliate. When I told my mother, she said, "Yes, but they do these things out of ignorance. You must not come down to their level. If you have to cast a stone, be sure to miss!"
In your biography, In Search of Greatness, *you mention the migration of your family from Mardin to Syria in 1922. You mentioned a strange wall you viewed on your journey. Could you tell me about that?*
Yes. We were told that we could leave Mardin, but could take nothing with us. We were compelled to travel by caravan, not by train. This was done intentionally by the Turks. They knew it would only be a matter of a few days' travel by train. By caravan, we could be bled to death at every stop by the sheiks in every

Turkish village. We were. They took our very last coins. At one village, the Turks made sure that we saw a special wall they had constructed. Its surface was covered with protruding skulls and ribs—bones of all sorts. There was no doubt that these had been human beings. The Turks took great joy in showing us this, hoping to instill fear with their barbaric wall. I cannot explain why— perhaps to record a last bitter memory of my country—I withdrew a paper and pencil and tried to draw the wall. I do not draw well at all, but I tried to sketch this terrible wall. One of the Turks saw me and shouted. Very quickly, I crumpled up the paper and threw it into a stream nearby, but it did not sink. It floated! The Turk ran to the stream, caught hold of the paper and held it up. Much shouting. I felt, because of my foolish act, that we were doomed. They took the paper to my father and, somehow, he managed to convince the Turks to let us continue. Later, I learned from my mother that it cost us our last silver coin.

Do you believe that what you endured as a child at the hands of the Turks may have been partly responsible for your entering an artistic career?

You know, I originally wanted to be a doctor.

You did?

Yes, for a very long time I had thought of being a doctor. But to return to your question, one cannot experience what I experienced and go untouched. It was a time of high emotion. These things that happened in Turkey, that is the old Turkey—I always make that qualification—certainly made me more aware of who I was and where I was. I think many things must happen to a person before he chooses his career. Certainly, there was always a strong strain of artistic expression in my family. My mother was well-read. My uncles were fine craftsmen, copiers of the Bible— what do you call it? Calligraphers—one produced fine, very fine illuminated manuscripts of parts of the Bible.

These were the uncles killed during the Turkish terror?

Yes.

How did you come to immigrate to Halifax, Nova Scotia, on New Year's eve in 1925?

My uncle Nakash, who was a photographer in Canada—a gentle,

understanding person—made all the arrangements. He wrote letters and helped with passports and offered me a home in the new world. Such a wonderful man. He took complete care of me when I arrived. He also made arrangements for me to study as an apprentice to the great Garo in Boston, Massachusetts.

That was John Garo?

Yes, he was known everywhere, and his studio had a grand salon atmosphere. All kinds of people came to visit with Garo—many celebrities.

You served as an apprentice to Garo from 1928 to 1931?

Yes, those were the years.

Garo had become an internationally-known portrait photographer by the time you met him in 1928, having taken photographs of President Coolidge and Secretary of the Navy, Charles Francis Adams. Was it when you were working with Garo that you decided to concentrate your photographic energies exclusively on world-renowned celebrities?

Everyone came to Garo's studio in Boston—writers, artists, singers. Oh, Garo loved singers. He had a beautiful bass voice and would break into a marvelous aria in the studio, particularly when noted singers were present. Then someone would decide to have a party and there would be a party during the evening. Wonderful parties. People like Arthur Fiedler came to Garo's studio. Being there and seeing these people was a momentous experience. I certainly became accustomed to celebrities at this time, and they intrigued me.

You have previously mentioned that Garo had a magnificent collection of 16-by-20-inch original negatives from prints. You have said that these gum arabic prints are still unmatched.

The gum arabic prints done by Garo are completely durable . . . they will never wear out. Garo worked only with available light, and for his prints, this kind of light was the best.

Do you use these techniques today at all?

No, never. This is a long, a very long and involved process. Sometimes it would take days to make such a print. Solutions had to be applied again and again until just the right texture was achieved. It is much too tedious to do today.

Why did you leave Garo?

He wanted me to continue with him, but I began to feel that available light was not enough. I wanted to work with artificial light, to create the same conditions available light could create, but achieve this with my own artificial light. Garo's photography was like a painting. It seemed to copy painting. I sought originality. A photographer who wants originality must not copy from anything. His work must be individualistic. Photography and painting are separate arts.

Speaking of techniques, there were many photographers developing their special techniques and styles during your years with Garo, such as Edward Steichen and Man Ray in Europe. What are your impressions of these men?

Man Ray is a wonderful artist. He was then, and has always been, considered an innovator, an improvisationalist. As such, he has made his kind of photography into an unusual and stimulating art. His work has always given me great joy.

As an innovator, of course, you are talking of his earliest beginnings in Paris, during the Twenties when he was involved in the Dadaist movement? [Dada was a quasi-literary artistic movement that practiced a sort of humorous nihilism in art, later commercialized by the Beats into an awkward brand of disenchantment literature and art.]

Yes, he would always involve himself in such enterprises.

Are you familiar with the incident where Man Ray was asked to make a movie by Tristan Tzara, founder of Dadaism?

[Eyes opening wide, curious] Noooo . . .

Ray told Tzara he did not know how to make a movie, but Tzara insisted that they have one for a Dada exhibit at a local theater in Paris. Ray then said he would try and make a movie by somehow attaching negatives together which were subsequently cranked through an improvised movie projector. The photos were all of dead insects and nuts and bolts Ray had collected in his Paris apartment, and the movie itself was extremely difficult to view. In fact, when the movie was shown, the audience was so infuriated with the film that they tore the seats from the theater and burned them in the street in protest.

Yousuf Karsh, the world's greatest portrait photographer, relaxing in his Ottawa, Canada home where only one photo adorns the walls.

As I have said, Man Ray is an innovator, but this is a negative reaction to his work. That has not been the case with most of what he has done, and that has been a positive and creative force. I am glad that you told me the story. I did not know it.

And Steichen?

[Folding his hands, almost a short, discernible nod of respect] Captain Steichen is an absolute master, a great artist. He is interested in all things living. The last time we were together, he was absorbed with the photography of flowers. Even the smallest daisy has beauty for him. His *Family of Man* is a classical study of human beings from all ways of life. He is a master.

You opened your own studio for the first time in Ottawa in 1932. Can you tell us your feelings about this?

It was very difficult at first—a struggle. I worked very hard, as anyone must work hard, but I knew what I wanted to do. My first wife, Solange, helped me in everything. It was at this time that I became interested in the little theater group in Ottawa. Solange introduced these people to me and we gave little theater parties.

Is the Solange Karsh Award made in connection with the theater groups in Ottawa?

Yes. You know that I lost my first wife to cancer some years ago. In her memory, the Solange Karsh Award was established. It is a medal executed by Philip Aziz to my specifications. One side of the medal has an engraving of Solange which is taken from my photograph of her. On the other side of the medal is the Canadian coat of arms, our adopted country. This prize is given to the author of the best one-act Canadian play. This is awarded through the Little Theater Workshop in Canada. And we give the author a small purse. It is not a lot, but something. There should always be a small purse. It is nice to have the medal, but it is also important that the author receive some sort of financial reward.

Of all the portraits you have taken, which do you believe to be the pivotal work upon which your reputation became established? Was it your portrait of Winston Churchill?

Yes, the Churchill.

Much has been written and said about this portrait—that you actually snatched or grabbed his cigar from his mouth and quickly

caught him in the belligerent pose you may have produced. Can
you tell us the real story here?

Telling that story has almost been the curse of my life. This
happened in 1941, just after Pearl Harbor had been bombed. The
Great Man was to come to Ottawa. Through my friend and patron,
William Lyon Mackenzie King, the prime minister of Canada, it
was arranged that I would photograph Churchill after his address
to the House of Commons. That was the speech in which Churchill
replied to the French generals who had predicted that "England
would have its neck wrung like a chicken." And Churchill replied
in his Canadian speech, "Some chicken, some neck!"

I had prepared to photograph Churchill in the speaker's cham-
ber, immediately after he finished with his speech to the House.
My equipment was all set up and then the door opened and he
walked in, arm-in-arm with Mackenzie King and others. I turned
on my floodlight. "What's this? What's this?" he demanded to
know. To my horror, no one had told him he was to have his portrait taken. I went to him and said, "Sir, I hope I will be fortunate
enough to make a portrait of you worthy of this historic occasion."
To make matters worse, everyone with him laughed. "Why was I
not told of this?"

He stared and then lit up a new cigar, puffing, puffing smoke
in a mischievous sort of way. "You may take one," he said. I
asked him to step forward into my lights and he did, but he *would*
not put down the cigar . . . puff, puff, puff. I brought forth an
ashtray, and said "Sir, would you, please?" He held tightly to the
cigar. "Will you please remove it, sir?" He held onto the cigar. I
felt that such a historic photo of Churchill on such an occasion
was best without the cigar. So I went back to my camera, checked
my lights, and removed the slide from the camera. I walked back
to him and, *very lightly*, removed the cigar from his lips saying
"Forgive me, sir." This was done almost with reverence, in a way
that I might remove something from your suit, something like . . .

Lint?

Yes, yes, lint. I took the picture, and he stood there looking
extremely belligerent, like he would devour me. After the picture
was taken, there was a deadly silence. No one spoke at all.

Churchill stared. He said, "You may take a second one." I took another picture of him smiling and being very gay. Then he walked over to me and shook my hand. "You can even make a roaring lion stand still to be photographed," he said.

In 1943 you took an unprecedented trip to London to photograph a host of personalities. Why, at this time, did you decide to make such a trip, especially to wartime London?

It was a rare opportunity. I realized that there were all those great personalities in one city and, perhaps, they might never be gathered together again. So, with the help of the Canadian government and others who arranged the passage I went to England. It was the hardest work of my life. You can imagine what it was like. One day with George Bernard Shaw . . . the next day with H. G. Wells . . . the next day with Noel Coward . . . 43 portraits in 60 days!

You also did portraits for a good many of the royalty . . . King George, King Haakon of Norway. The king of Norway was extremely tall, a giant. How did you photograph him? Sitting down?

No, but he was very tall. He wore an admiral's uniform. I never have anyone just sit down. I take the portrait naturally, as they seem best.

Many of your later portraits—Robert Frost, Helen Keller, John L. Lewis—all seem to possess a grass-roots feeling, a common-man expression. How did you achieve this?

Only Lewis gave me that feeling, that common man thing. Helen Keller and Robert Frost were much more expressive, different. Lewis was rough, rough-hewn, and his face said it.

Your portrait of Jean Sibelius was particularly moving, with eyes almost closed, his arm up at an angle that suggests that he is about to begin conducting his own composition.

Sibelius, wonderful man that he was, was very old when I did his portrait, 91. His hands shook terribly with palsy. In the portrait he is really steadying his hand by holding onto his . . . he is holding his lapel [Karsh grabbed his own lapel to demonstrate]. The expression on his face came after I told him that during the war the Finns working in the fields slowed down. The production necessary to the fighting men was very slow, and so authorities had his, Sibelius', *Finlandia* played so that the workers could hear. When they heard this, their beloved *Finlandia*, the great music of their own Sibelius, their production doubled almost immediately. Sibelius was so moved by this story that he closed his eyes and I took his portrait.

It was reported that you once said you disliked taking the portraits of actors; that you preferred doing musicians.

No, I did not say I disliked taking the photographs of actors. They are not always quite at ease, natural. They seem to feel they must pose. Some are unnatural, and it is difficult to portray their genuine selves. Musicians, on the other hand, are very easy. I have just photographed Pablo Casals for the second time. He is extremely natural before the camera.

One of the actors you photographed was Humphrey Bogart. How did you get along with Bogie?

He was splendid, a very thoughtful and warm-hearted person. The only thing was that everything was all right as long as I kept up with him on the drinking. I showed him my book, the one with the portrait of King George, and he called to his English butler. "Hey, come 'ere. I wantcha to meet the guy who took the picture of your King!"

And Ingrid Bergman?

A great person. She has had her troubles, and when I made her photograph, she was having great personal difficulties. But she patiently worked with me, and some time later she wrote to us in Little Wings and told us that it was her favorite portrait.

You even photographed Boris Karloff. What was it like to photograph a man who has played the most evil villains in films?

Oh, he was a very sensitive man. A creative and kind man. I think a man like Karloff, a person who is so gentle and understands life so well, is the only kind of person who could understand evil and play it so well.

Your portrait of Admiral "Bull" Halsey has a great deal of humor behind it, I believe.

Ah, yes, the admiral. He appeared before the camera in civilian clothes. I said, "Here you are an admiral and there is no uniform. You should have the uniform" "I have no uniform," he said. We had made the arrangements to have uniforms there, and I told the admiral that they were available and that I believed the publishers of his book would want to have his portrait in the uniform for the book's jacket. So he put on the uniform, but the battle cap did not fit. I said, "How much would this cap be worth?" "About seven dollars," and I cut the back of the cap so that it would fit. After all, we were only taking the front. That's all people would see on the book jacket.

Your portrait of Ernest Hemingway is considered to be the best in the world of this great author. Can you tell us what your experiences were with Hemingway?

I went to Havana, Cuba, to photograph Hemingway with much cooperation from the officials there. Hemingway was living with Miss Mary in their home. When I met him, I found him to be very, very shy. To this date, he is the shyest man I have ever photographed. He was extremely courteous and very kind to both me and my wife. I had read much about him, as I do with all of those who I am going to photograph.

I have heard that you also study press photographs of your subject as part of your research. Am I correct?

Yes. And I had read that Hemingway loved daquiris. So when I went to the house, and he asked me if I would like something to drink, I said, "Yes, please, a daquiri." "In the morning?" he asked. I told him that I had read that he liked daquiris. He said that was true, but what he meant by something to drink was coffee or tea.

How many days did it take to do the Hemingway portrait?

Two. He had asked us to dine with him the evening of the first day. We agreed that we would. That night I was in the Floridita Bar, Hemingway's favorite bar in Havana, where he was known for his daquiri drinks, and a small revolution broke out . . . right in the bar! Bullets were flying about! Yousuf Karsh was flat on his face on the floor. It was quite an experience, and I did not feel like going to Hemingway's home for dinner, and I thought that he would not be up to it either with all the shooting in the streets. I called him the next morning and he said he was very disappointed that we had not come to dinner. "But, didn't you hear the noise, the shooting! There was a revolution going on!" I said.

"Oh," he said. "That happens all the time."

That day we worked many hours and I could not get Hemingway in the mood for the portrait. It finally became necessary for me to ask Miss Mary and my wife to leave the room. Everyone had to leave. It was the only way. Then he put on a beautiful sweater, a special hand-woven turtleneck sweater with a felt front. This sweater was a "gift" from Christian Dior of Paris. Hemingway told me about having dinner once in Paris, and among the guests at the party was the fashion designer, Christian Dior. Dior looked down the table at Hemingway and said, "Hemingway, I have a wonderful idea. I am going to make you a special creation, a great sweater. It will be specially knitted and it will come up very high on your neck and it will be beautiful." Hemingway looked up from his meal and said, "So knit the sweater." This Christian Dior sweater was waiting for the Hemingways when they returned from Paris and there was also a bill. Miss Mary later said that the Hemingways went without their household money for a week to pay for it. [This sweater is worn in the most famous of all Hemingway portraits, done by Karsh.]

Did his putting on the sweater make things easier for the portrait work?

It seemed to relax him. Also, I learned that he liked a special kind of wine, chilled, at the time of the sitting. He would drink a glass of it and I would have half a glass. He would drink another glass and I would take another half a glass. Finally, he settled back and completely relaxed. It was then that I took the portrait. As he was sitting there, and we talked, I noticed that everything about him was big, large. He had especially large shoes. His feet were very big. He was a very sad, melancholy man, but he had a wonderful face—and that magnificent beard.

Did Hemingway ever tell you what he thought of this portrait?

Miss Mary wrote to us in Little Wings after Ernest's death and told us that he always thought the Karsh portrait to be his favorite.

You have photographed three Catholic Popes—Pope Pius, Pope John, and Pope Paul. In which way did you find these men different?

Pope Pius was very aloof, an intellectual. A great leader of his church, but remote. Pope John was very . . . down-to-earth, a man of the people . . . such a warm and friendly man. [In the *Karsh Portfolio*, Pope John is quoted as saying, "I wish you to enter into your diary that you have had the longest visit with Pope John to date." After the Karsh portrait was taken, Pope John smiled and repeated, *Bene, bene, bene* . . .] Pope Paul was a combination of both Pius and John. But I shall never forget John.

Tell us about your experience with Nikita Khrushchev. You did his portrait in a private dasha [small home].

I believe it was the first time anyone from outside Russia was permitted to photograph members of the Presidium . . . formal portraits. The Russians were very kind to us. I thought it might be best if Khrushchev were photographed in a fur coat. I asked if he would put one on. "Well," he explained, "at this time of year [it was spring] there just is not a fur coat available in the whole of Moscow." I mentioned to someone representing the government that it was too bad that even the Premier of Russia could not obtain a fur coat. Miraculously, a fur coat appeared almost in minutes. Khrushchev put the coat on, and also a head sweater which is shaped like a sock. It reminds me of a sock you put on your face and only the face is outside. This is the way I took his portrait. "I must escape this Russian leopard," Khrushchev said, "or it will devour me!" [Karsh then explained that he asked if he might photograph the entire executive membership of the Presidium. He was informed that this would be impossible.] However, the very next day, with Khrushchev himself making the introductions and bringing them into the area where my equipment was set up, the entire executive membership of the Presidium marched in and I took all of their portraits.

Your portrait of President Kennedy shows the president with his hands folded as if in prayer . . .

That was a natural gesture on his part. He was a very easy person to photograph. His portrait was taken in the Vice-President's office. I set up my equipment there. I reminded him that the portrait was to be in color and that his tie was not at all good for such a portrait. So he took *my* tie and I took his.

Did you keep the tie?

[Smiling] No.

Your photograph of Lyndon Johnson was taken four days after President Kennedy's death. How did he seem to you at this time?

It was a trying time for everyone. The very day that I went to photograph him, the Kennedy family was leaving. He told me that he might have to excuse himself to make his goodbyes. He excused himself three times.

One of your most interesting portraits is that of the Spanish painter, Joan Miró. There is an innocence, a joy in this new portrait that is almost childlike.

[Karsh's face broke into a wide smile] Miró is that kind of person—easy-going, deeply appreciative of life. A happy man who is also a great artist. Miró's portrait was accomplished in a matter of hours.

In your lighting, do you generally employ a certain number of strobes and flood lights in fixed positions?

Generally a certain number is used. The positions vary.

I have noticed that in your Churchill portrait, there is a small radiance of light coming from behind.

That was intentional. I thought it would give proper contrast and create the proper shadows. It was a small light.

And you work with shadows a great deal.

Why not? Half our lives are lived in shadows. It is only natural that they appear . . . in my portraits.

How many assistants do you use when taking a portrait?

One, only one.

Do you process your own photographs?

Not anymore, but I give the personnel at my studio in Ottawa complete directions at each phase of the development. I oversee everything and all processing is done according to my specifications.

It has been suggested by several photographers that you have some sort of secret process for achieving those marvelous tones of contrast in your portraits. Would you care to share this darkroom "secret"?

[Breaking into a broad grin] Perhaps I should not! But, no, of course, there is no special secret. It comes from my work, my original photograph. It is there, inside the photograph, and it is what I see.

You are noted for your encouragement to young photographers. Your home was once invaded by a host of 50 of them from Ohio State. What is the primary question they generally ask of you?

What is the quickest way to fame. The short-cut, you see. And the answer for all is that there is none. It takes much time—years —and struggle to establish the photographer's art.

The Karsh photograph of Hemingway, purported to be Hemingway's favorite portrait. "He is the shyest man I have ever photographed," said Karsh of the great author. (© Karsh, Ottawa, from his book *Karsh Portraits*)

Dorothy Parker,
A Wit for the Ages

Originality in writing style and inventive thought was vigorously abundant in the work of Dorothy Parker, coupled with a lifestyle that would make any number of today's women writers appear anemic, vapid and enslaved by the dictates of this era's sexual separatism. Mrs. Parker was a pathfinder for women writers to be sure, but, moreover, she emerged as an individual literary force whose sardonic wit captured the follies and foibles of departing love.

Mrs. Parker produced marvelous and consistently fresh verse which was collected into several volumes, including the much-treasured *Enough Rope* and *Sunset Gun*, the former containing two universally quoted passages, the first on suicide, "Resume," the second on girls who wear glasses, "News Item." Her poignant short-story collections, *After Such Pleasures* and *Here Lies*, offer classic tales of disenchantment, notably "Big Blonde" and "A Telephone Call."

As a critic, Dorothy Parker was terse, devastating and incomparable. When reviewing one unsuccessful Broadway

To encourage more visitors to her office Dorothy Parker had a sign painted on her door. (Illustration by Al Hirschfield)

play, Mrs. Parker's razor-sharp remark concerned the acting ability of a young Katherine Hepburn. Hepburn's acting, wrote Dorothy Parker, "ran the whole gamut of emotions from A to B."

Caustic, clever, always creative, Mrs. Parker remains a startling innovator whose style and stories are imitated to this day. She was also a madcap lady who enjoyed life and had fun, a lot of fun.

The following profile, originally entitled *A Nosegay for Mrs. Parker*, appeared in *Omnibus Magazine*, August 1967, following her death in New York on June 7, 1967.

When Frank Crowninshield, publisher and mentor of the old lace-curtain *Vogue* before the twittering Twenties twinkled, paid a dreamy-eyed girl with bangs $12 for a small verse, it is doubtful that he could have foreseen the unleashing of a literary whirling dervish, Dorothy Rothschild Parker.

The verses of Dorothy Parker, like most female writers of the day, followed in the delicate footsteps of Edna St. Vincent Millay, but Crowninshield's $12 worth of print bought him a storehouse of exciting talent. To compound his Maecenas role, Crowninshield hired Mrs. Parker for *Vogue*'s staff at $10 a week, which he was later to regret but much to the delight of humor fans everywhere.

In early *Vogue*'s editorial labyrinth, the small, darkly attractive girl churned out captions like "This little pink dress will win you a beau." Then Crowninshield moved her onto the staff of his super-sophisticated *Vanity Fair*. Mrs. Parker worked there four long, fanciful years, taking over the drama criticism from P. G. Wodehouse.

There was plenty of fine and funny literary company for her. The great humorist, Robert Benchley, was managing editor and Robert E. Sherwood, who was to write *The Petrified Forest* and win three Pulitzer Prizes, was the drama editor, Dorothy Parker's editor. It was at *Vanity Fair* that Mrs. Parker blossomed into a lethal wit and full-time prankster.

During the First World War, a *Vanity Fair* editor, Albert Lee, had a map over his desk which was dotted with flags indicating where the troops were fighting. His penchant for following the boys "over there" was too much for devilish Dorothy.

"Since I didn't have anything better to do, I'd get up half an hour early and go down and change his flags," she later recalled. Then, "Lee would come in, look at his map, and he'd get very serious about spies, shout, and spend his morning moving his little pins back into positions."

A thick streak of the macabre was ingrained in Mrs. Parker's nature, undoubtedly encouraged by her editorial henchman, Benchley. Both of them subscribed to undertaking magazines, their favorites being *The Casket* and *Sunnyside.* "Steel yourself—" she remembered "*Sunnyside* had a joke column called 'From Grave to Gay.' "

Robert E. Sherwood was close to seven feet tall. Just as James Joyce was terrified of any size dog (he had been chewed upon by a mongrel pooch as a child in Dublin), Sherwood feared midgets. Since *Vanity Fair*'s offices were across from the Hippodrome, the midgets appearing in the acts there constantly plagued Sherwood with, "How's the weather up there?"

"Walk down the street with me," he would ask Mrs. Parker and Benchley, and they would leave their jobs and run interference against the bevy of little people. "I can't tell you," Mrs. Parker rejoiced, "we had more fun . . . ."

The fun came to a jolting halt when Mrs. Parker "fixed" three plays, panning them so adroitly that her reviews became mortal wounds. One review, swimming in page space, simply and smashingly stated, "*The House Beautiful* is the play lousy."

In 1920, Mrs. Parker's review of Somerset Maugham's *Caesar's Wife* tore into the acting ability of Florenz Ziegfeld's wife, Billie Burke. "Miss Burke," Mrs. Parker wrote, "is at her best in her more serious moments; in her desire to convey the girlishness of the character, she plays her lighter scenes rather as if she were giving an impersonation of Eva Tanguay [a then popular burlesque star]." Theatrical potentate Ziegfeld exploded. He threatened to tear apart the offices of *Vanity Fair* and remove his advertising from all Conde Nast publications.

Crowninshield did what Alexander Woollcott's *New York*

Times editors had refused to do when the Shubert impresarios threatened loss of advertising for Woollcott's consistent damning of their plays: Mrs. Parker was fired from *Vanity Fair*.

Benchley and Sherwood, in a typical act of comraderie which blessed their enviable literary milieu, rose up mightily and also resigned from the magazine. The three made cardboard chevrons marked "Fired" and wore them in a parade about *Vanity Fair*'s offices and throughout Manhattan. But they never worried about jobs in those saxophone years. If you had talent, you would make out. It might have been a little rougher for Benchley, who had to feed a family, but Benchley, like Mrs. Parker, Sherwood, Woollcott, and F.P.A. (Franklin Pierce Adams) moved as the whim urged. (Benchley once set fire to Teddy Roosevelt, Jr., on Fifth Avenue when the ex-president's son complained of the chill in the air, but that is another story.)

Mrs. Parker and Benchley rented a loft above the old Metropolitan Opera House as an "office" and became free-lance writers. The office was so small that Mrs. Parker quipped, "an inch smaller and it would have been adultery. We had *Parkbench* for a cable address, but no one ever sent us one."

In the *Parkbench* days, Mrs. Parker and Benchley would frequent the Algonquin hotel. There, in the middle of a small dining room, the notorious Round Table of famous writers and critics and literary quacks held court, dominated by the humorously-vicious Alexander Woollcott, who discovered the place and made it headquarters because its homemade apple pie suited his distinguished palate.

The Round Table was a beehive of invective, witticism, and barbs—a murderous crossfire in a critical no-man's-land into which any fledgling writer would be loath to enter. Some visitors like the young James Thurber, chaperoned by Harold Ross, or the aspiring actress Tallulah Bankhead (called the "Scavenger" by Woollcott), or Edna Ferber were reduced to silence or near tears under the savage onslaughts of the hyper-critical quipsters.

According to Mrs. Parker, a regular in attendance "[George S.] Kaufman was there. I guess he was sort of funny. Mr. Sherwood and Mr. Benchley went when they had a nickel. Franklin P.

Adams, whose column was widely read by people who wanted to write, would sit in occasionally. And Harold Ross, the *New Yorker* editor. He was a professional lunatic, but I don't know if he was a great man. He had a profound ignorance. On one of Mr. Benchley's manuscripts he wrote on the margin opposite 'Andromache,' 'Who he?' Mr. Benchley wrote back, 'You keep out of this.' The only one with stature who came to the Round Table was Heywood Broun."

Broun, a star columnist for the old *New York World*, was bounced by editor Herbert Bayard Swope because of his constant dwelling upon the Sacco-Vanzetti case. Swope warned him, after countless Broun columns on the case had appeared, of what might happen. Broun ignored him. The next day when the Round Table convened, they opened up *The New York World* to Broun's column. Instead of finding the much-vaunted editorial writer's column, the readers were met with: "The *World* has decided to dispense with the services of Heywood Broun." That's how Broun discovered he was out of a job.

Alexander Woollcott and Dorothy Parker were intimate friends, although Woollcott must have worn down the edges of that friendship with his unchecked barbs. A tantrum tosser when he lost at cards, Woollcott usually played poker at the Algonquin with Kaufman, Broun, Ross, F.P.A., Frank Sullivan and Benchley. Mrs. Parker was the only female allowed to attend these poker pogroms, but Woollcott insisted that she sit away from the table. She could make comments only if they were tolerable to Sir Oracle, Woollcott.

One evening, Woollcott grew impatient with Kaufman, who took his own good time deciding on his bet. He smiled wryly and took more time as Woollcott's owlish face puffed out in anger. When he could bear it no longer, Woollcott blurted, "Play, c'mon, play, Christkiller."

This Woollcottian affront, although Kaufman and he had traded tongue lashings for years in friendly jousts, appeared to end their friendship. Kaufman put his cards down quietly and, with solemn face, arose from the table. He looked briefly at Dorothy Parker, who was half Jewish, for a response. Then he turned to his antagonist. "Woollcott," he said slowly, "I have taken your abuse for years, but that last remark was the final insult." He began to walk toward the door. Then, he turned in a grandiloquent gesture and said, "I am going out that door . . . and . . . I expect Mrs. Parker to follow me . . . half way!"

When Benchley departed from the *Parkbench* office, Mrs. Parker grew lonely. No one visited her small domain. She hit upon a scheme that would provide instant company. She had a sign painted on her office door. It read: "MEN."

Alexander Woollcott's outward attitude was blatantly waspish; underneath was a quivering, sentimental nature. But his wit could often prove exasperating. When Mrs. Parker remarried, she made the fatal error of citing Woollcott as a reference for financial reliability to a New York department store. She and her new husband, Alan Campbell, regretted this when they received a copy of his endorsement, which read: "Mr. Alan Campbell, the present husband of Dorothy Parker, has given my name as a reference in his attempt to open an account at your store. We all hope that you will extend this credit to him. Surely Dorothy Parker's position in American letters is such as to make shameful the petty refusals which she and Alan have encountered at many hotels, restaurants and department stores. What if you never get paid? Why shouldn't you stand your share of the expense?" Such impish double-dealing should have been expected from a man who bluntly told her literary majesty, Gertrude Stein, "It's obvious that you have not been in New York long enough to know that I'm never contradicted!"

Mrs. Parker once showed up on Woollcott's private Vermont island, Bomoseen. She declared herself penniless.

"Here you are and here you stay," Woollcott exclaimed. (He exclaimed everything.)

Three weeks later, after compelling her to play constant rounds of croquet (Woollcott would strike anyone with a mallet who made him look poor) and endure his all-through-the-night "brain twisters" game, the critic turned to her and said, "Say, isn't it about time you were leaving?"

"On what?" Mrs. Parker asked.

Dorothy Parker at age 70 in 1963: "Men seldom make passes at girls who wear glasses."

Woollcott, whose income was gigantic compared to that of most critics, gave her a train ticket and $2.50 in cold, hard cash.

As the roaring Twenties roared, Dorothy Parker gave little credence to the built-in tragedy of the "Lost Generation." She later commented, "We all said, 'Whee! We're Lost!' " The serious writers—Fitzgerald, Hemingway, Dos Passos—were dealing with disheartened young men and women in a vast time of social change. "Many of my friends started to disappear into the dark maw of violence," Scott Fitzgerald wrote in *The Crack-Up*, and he illustrated by citing suicides, which somehow, in the Twenties, seemed romantic to some. Mrs. Parker rammed that romance into parody with these lines from "Resumé": *Razors pain you;/ Rivers are damp;/ Acids stain you;/ And drugs cause cramp./ Guns aren't lawful;/ Nooses give; /Gas smells awful;/ You might as well live.*

She also documented her bittersweet society in her classic story, "Big Blonde," which, along with "A Telephone Call" and "Soldiers of the Republic," established her as an imaginative and perceptive writer.

In 1931, Mrs. Parker was reviewing books for Harold Ross's *New Yorker*, signing them, "Constant Reader." She pulled a bon mot on her own bon mot when, reviewing one of A. A. Milne's more banal and sugary works, she remarked, "At this point Tonstant Weader fwowed up."

Although she always enjoyed the company of men, Mrs. Parker was known throughout the land as a man-baiter in her prose and poetry, most decidedly her poetry. The last stanza from "Men: A Hate Song," proudly printed in the revised *Vanity Fair* edition now on sale to collectors, is indicative of her special technique: *There are the ones/ Who are Simply Steeped in Crime/ They tell you how they haven't been to bed/ For four nights./ They frequent those dramas/ Where the only good lines/ Are those of the chorus./ They stagger from one cabaret to another/ And they give you the exact figures of their gambling debts/ They hint darkly at the terrible part/ That alcohol plays in their lives/ And they shake their heads/ And say heaven must decide what is going to become of them—/ I wish I were Heaven!*

When the Round Table began to split up, many writers retired to country homes, others to Europe. Dorothy Parker went where most writers of the Thirties were expected to go: Hollywood, to write for the flickers.

"Now that you've become Hollywood's pet, you'll never come back," Alexander Woollcott wailed. And until she returned to New York to write reviews for *Esquire*, Mrs. Parker did not.

For a while, she lived in the Garden of Allah, a strange Hollywood motel without cars where Bob Benchley and F. Scott Fitzgerald were living. It was here that she formed a deep friendship with Fitzgerald, the golden-tongued literary spokesman of their generation.

Mrs. Parker remembered his early death at 43: "When he died no one went to the funeral, not a single soul came, or even sent a flower. I said 'Poor son of a bitch,' a quote right out of *The Great Gatsby*, and everyone thought it was another wisecrack. But it was said in dead seriousness."

When Dorothy Parker herself died, some of the more uninspired obituary writers dismissed her out of hand, saying she was merely "part of a wild crowd" whose "days were gone forever," one anonymous sniper stating that "her work was only of a minor nature." That claim, of course, has been proven false. Mrs. Parker's poems and stories live today in permanent printed collections, and, more important, inside living hearts which revel in the lady's long laughter.

Willie "The Actor" Sutton, Bank Robber

In the world of cold, cold crime there was never a more infamous bank robber and burglar than William Francis Sutton (1901-80), Willie "The Actor" as he was known on the front pages and in police blotters. He was also one of the great escape artists in American penal history. Sutton, who spent most of his adult life behind bars, escaped Sing Sing on December 12, 1932, by picking a series of locks and then scaling the prison's walls. He spent a year (1944-45) tunneling out of Pennsylvania's Eastern State Penitentiary in Philadelphia only to be apprehended moments after he jumped out of the hole. He escaped from the same prison—he called it his "masterpiece"—on February 9, 1947, dropping over the prison's 40-foot wall with extension ladders taken from the institution's basement, using a blinding snowstorm as a cover.

Sutton was a man obsessed with robbing banks, and he is credited with robbing almost 100 of them. "Why did I rob banks?" he once stated. "Because I enjoyed it. I loved it. I was more alive when I was inside a bank, robbing it, than any

A cell block in Sing Sing in 1932 when Willie Sutton escaped from this maximum security prison.

other time in my life. I enjoyed everything about it so much
that one or two weeks later I'd be out looking for the next
job. But to me, the money was the chips, that's all. The win-
nings. I kept robbing banks when, by all logic, it was foolish,
when it could cost me far more than I could possibly gain."

The way in which Sutton robbed banks made him unique
in the annals of the underworld. He was called "the actor"
because of his ability to assume disguises; he actually made
up his face as would an actor before a performance each time
he struck. And according to the records, as well as Willie's
own insistent admission, he never hurt a soul while performing a bank robbery—a fact that did not ameliorate his actions
but did explain his practical character. Sutton, who spent 50
years as a thief, was released from prison in 1969. He lived
to write a bestseller, *Where the Money Was, The Memoirs of
a Bank Robber*, about which he jocularly stated: "It was a
very moral book. The message it imparted was that crime
doesn't pay . . . but writing about it does."

In the following interview, conducted for the author's
syndicated column, "Crime Journal," on September 17, 1976,
Sutton the innovator recalled a career in crime that was
unique but painful and full of self-punishment. By then
Willie had spent a half dozen years lecturing delinquent
youths on the self-destruction such a career would always
bring. He was not proud of the career but rather talked of it
as if observing the ghost of his other self, witnessing his own
infamy much like Scrooge looking backward with a shudder
at "the chains he himself had forged in life."

Your book Where The Money Was—*was this really something
that you wanted to do, to kind of tell all, or was it an avenue to
make a little money?*

A lot of people have asked me if I have any guilt complexes
concerning the money I robbed from banks. So I told them no,
but my greatest concern is these young people today, who may try
to emulate my acts. I think the book contains a message to show
how futile a life of crime really is. My life has been thoroughly
wasted.

You were in prison how long? Thirty some years?

About 33 years. About half of my adult life. You hear people say that I'll do this and I'll suffer the consequences, but that isn't true in life, because every act a person commits, reflects upon many other people—family, friends, neighbors, or anybody who might have known him. So these people who think that they are being tough or being brave by saying they'll suffer the consequences are not really telling the truth.

Isn't there a feeling, Willie, in the criminal business that if you took a fall, if you went to prison, it was part of the business? And you accepted it as such.

That's very true, because I, myself, accepted that same philosophy. I never made any excuses to anybody for my crimes. I always believed that I was up against . . . that I was actually one man against the Establishment, I guess, in a lot of instances. I knew that if I was arrested or caught or convicted, I knew that I would go to jail for a certain specified number of years. So it's a philosophy that a more intelligent person accepts. There are too many people trying to rationalize their behavior. They can't accept the guilt themselves and they try to blame others for their downfall. But I was never in that category of people. I always accepted what came to me as being my just desserts.

When you were in the business, did you consider yourself a professional bank robber or bank burglar, which?

I considered myself a professional bank robber because I robbed about 100 banks. The only thing I have out of this whole thing is that I acquired a very intensive and extensive knowledge of people in prison. I used my time to the best of my ability. I studied all the things that I thought would be beneficial to me.

What do you mean you studied? Casing banks?

Well you're talking about outside. I'm talking about inside and what I learned from the 33 years I put in prison. But outside I don't think anybody ever put into crime the time and the thought and the planning that I did. I used to plan these crimes or perpetrate these crimes or do something in relation to the crimes that took up my whole time. I was completely absorbed in it.

You blueprinted every job?

I blueprinted every job and that's the difference. People ask me today what's the difference between these modern bank robbers and me. Well, the modern bank robber sets out to terrorize people and to put fear into them. Now my modus operandi was entirely opposite of that. I set out to instill confidence in people —to give them the confidence to know . . .

While you were taking the money?

Yes. I would tell them that it wasn't their money and so forth. But what I tried to do, I tried to assure them from the very outset, that they weren't in any kind of trouble and I asked them to cooperate with me.

Now what kind of mental state were you in before you pulled off one of these robberies? Were you hyped up? Were you excited at the prospect of the robbery you were about to commit?

Well, yes. I was. I was naturally excited about the thing.

I'm not talking about fear.

About the planning and the actual perpetration of the crimes. I naturally was very excited about it.

Were these "kicks" for you?

I would just say that I was very excited and I was exhilarated, naturally, after the commission of the crime which went off, you know, pretty good. I looked upon the success of the thing as the outcome of the plan. See, by planning these things, I eliminated about 95 percent of the risk of robbing a bank. That is, I took into consideration all the unforeseen circumstances that might arise on a job. Now rarely did I show a pistol. They knew I had a pistol.

But you did use a pistol?

Well I didn't use it. I carried a pistol.

And a machinegun at one time?

That's right. At one time I tried that out and I figured it was too much of a terrorizing feature and I dropped that completely right away.

Let me ask you something important about using weapons in a robbery. If you were confronted with a situation I would think that if you had to use that weapon, you would have. Correct?

In my own mind I would say no, I think you're wrong. I was a very athletic person. And I took very good care of myself and I learned judo. And I always had confidence that if anybody gave me any trouble that I could disarm them or put them out of play by my physical prowess, rather than a gun. And it may seem strange to you or to anybody, that at the age of 75 years of age, I can say to you, that never in my life have I fired a pistol—not even on a target range.

Were the weapons that you used loaded?

They were loaded, yes. They were. But they were more or less used for effect.

You're saying they were for display only? Is that it?

That's right. If I had to display them or if those in the bank knew they were in my pocket and so forth, it had a psychological effect upon them.

Now, the sobriquet, the nickname "The Actor," this comes from your penchant for making yourself up in disguises. You did things with your face. You assumed different identities. Let me ask you, did you have a make-up kit?

Oh, yes. I had greasepaint and everything. I had a professional make-up kit.

Give me some examples of what you would do in making your disguises?

I would use various types of mustaches, for instance. I'd put on a small goatee, or I would have a hollowed out cork and I would wipe my nose.

You would put the corks in your nostrils?

That's right, and have them hollowed out so that I could breathe through them. And I used different colored dyes on my hair. I was blonde, I was red-headed, I was black-headed. I used every kind of dye known. And, by the way, I still use that dye if you've noticed, that's that Grecian Formula Sixteen and much better.

But for different reasons.

Yeah, that's right, for *much better* different reasons.

And you used uniforms, too, in your robberies?

I used all kinds of uniforms, policemen's uniforms, postmen's uniforms, firemen's uniforms.

This gave you easier access to the bank?

That's right. See, everything was deceptive. I had to get into the bank before the employees got in there. Now the first man in there, I would have a talk with him. He would tell me his name and I had a number of chairs. I knew how many people were going to come into that bank.

What would you tell the bank guard?

Well, first I would disarm him.

You were dressed as a policeman. What did you do—knock on the door of the bank?

I rang the bell.

Before the bank opened?

Yes. I would use various excuses: "I'd like to use the men's room," and so forth, or, "Is everything all right? I'd like to step in for a few minutes," and so forth. A uniform is a very disarming thing and if a cop tells you to move you might resent it, but you're going to move. I'd get the first man. I would tell him: "This is a hold-up—now this money doesn't belong to you. I'm not here to hurt you or hurt anybody. If you will please cooperate with me, nobody is going to get hurt and nobody is going to lose their money."

Would you tell this person these words in the same quiet tone of voice you're using now?

Yes. In an explanatory way. So I would tell him: "Now look. When the next man comes in you explain what this is, that it's a robbery." You see, people were walking in to what amounted to an ambush. They didn't know a robbery was going on. So, they'd walk in and I'd take them by the arm and say, "Do you mind sitting over there with Mr. Foley? He wants to tell you something." They'd walk over and they'd sit down and that's when Mr. Foley or whoever it might be would explain that it was a robbery and that I wasn't there to hurt them, that the money didn't belong to them and so forth.

In other words, you were really mostly concerned with the bank guard first and, once you had cowed him, you allowed him to do your work for you by explaining that there was a bank robbery going on?

Sutton (seated at right, coatless) in custody in 1952, being asked if the guns in the detective's hands and the wad of hundred dollar bills were on his person when arrested. (They were.)

Right. And when they saw that somebody was there that they knew and that they weren't hurt, that had a psychological effect. The guy thinks, well, look, he's all right. So he walks over and sits down quietly.

How did you develop that kind of approach?

I studied psychology in prison for a while. And I also, later on, I worked six years for a psychiatrist. He used to bring me in a lot of books, psychiatric books.

This was in prison?

Yes. I studied political science. I read all of the great books of literature. And I amassed quite a knowledge in my years in prison because I never wasted them. They have a saying in prison, "Don't serve time; make time serve you." I tried to follow that. I've seen a lot of people in prison who didn't do very much with their minds and go what they call "stir-crazy."

When you became Prisoner #84599 in Sing Sing, for the first time, what started to happen to your identity? Did you alter your habits, your speech, your way of thinking?

No, not when I first went to prison. That was a very harrowing experience for me. You see, that prison [Sing Sing] was about 125 years old at the time. This was my first conviction.

Warden Lewis Lawes was there at the time?

That's right. The cells were almost indescribable. They weren't flat walls or flat ceilings. They were jagged rocks pointing into your cell. And the cells were extremely small in width. Your bed was just a little thing that you hung up and you lowered at night to sleep on. It was steel lattice work. You had a mattress, but that all folded into the bed.

And it had a privy?

No, you had a bucket. You had an iron bucket; each morning you had to take it out and empty it, and wash it. But when this bed was down in the cell, you had to go in sideways in order to actually get into the cell. And I often think to myself that if they put anybody in there, let's say some of these young people today, and put them in there for 15 or 20 days and then turn them out in the street, there wouldn't be any criminals anymore. It would put such a fear into them. But then after . . .

We're talking about one prisoner to a cell, this is the old Sing Sing.

That's right. That's the way it is in New York State. Always one to a cell. They don't double up. But today all these prisons are overcrowded, greatly overcrowded, and half of the prisoners, I guess, are drug addicts.

You stated several times in the past that you always distrusted partners, especially since they repeatedly led to your capture. Why then did you continue to link up with partners? Was it that you really needed them for the job? Or was it because partners gave you a sense of security in having someone else involved with you?

It was necessary to work with a partner. I'll tell you why. I could have maybe done a few smaller bank jobs, and I could only get a certain limited amount of money. But when I worked with one partner, I could take a much larger bank and if I worked with two partners, which I did on only one or two occasions, I could cover an immense area in the bank, like a mezzanine and so forth in the bank. If you had three men, you could cover everything. Whereas, with two, you would be one short. In a lot of instances I had to put these men close to the front door, and go into the rear of the bank where the vault was, so naturally I would leave the employees with my partner, while I went to get the money out of the vaults.

So it was really an expediency. You had to have partners to be able to pull—

It was a necessity, yes. If I wanted to make money.

You really didn't start off as a bank robber. You started off as a bank burglar.

That's right. One of the first jobs I ever did, was when I was about ten years old. I burglarized a small department store. That was a small neighborhood department store. By using the word "department store," you may get the idea it was a very large place. But it wasn't. It was a very small place and I took some money out of the cash registers. The first bank I did was with an acetylene torch. All of these things came together, the way I lived. For instance, I worked in a shipyard and I learned how to cut metal. I was very good at it. And I also worked in places where I had access to burglar alarms. And naturally all these things were done in an honest and legal way. But later on, they all merged into a plan. In one burglary I committed I encountered a lot of difficulty because I had to get through a concrete floor that was much thicker than I had assumed it would be.

How thick was it?

About four feet thick, I guess. So I had special drills and everything with me but it took longer than I had anticipated, and when I got in there, I was rushed, so I had to set something up so that I couldn't be seen from the street while I worked on the side of the vault. Well, the employees started coming, so I had to get out and I did. I got out. But later on, it dawned on me that if I had some kind of a pistol or something, I could have just let them in, and I could have continued on that job; I only had about ten more minutes' work with the torch and I would have had the money. So all of these things came together. And out of that grew this plan of mine, to get in a bank before the employees got in. To disarm the alarms, the various types of alarms they had, to protect myself against anybody stepping on a button or pushing a button. This whole thing merged together from a lot of honest toil.

You did your research and then finally, I assume, the methodology took care of itself.

That's right.

You obviously couldn't handle the situation without going into armed robbery, because that's exactly what it turned into.

That's right.

Let me ask you, Willie, as an inmate in various prisons, was the thought of escape in your mind from the first? Was that in your mind the first day, for instance, that you entered prison?

Yes, yes.

Right from the beginning?

Right from the very beginning. I'll tell you the reason how that started. When I was 29 years of age, the judge sentenced me to 30 years for a crime because they had what they called Senator Baum's law in New York and they were mandatory sentences. The

Willie Sutton in an interview, 1974: He spent half his adult life behind bars.

judge had no authority to sentence you to less, like if you were a
second offender you got 30 years for robbery and that was it. If
you were a fourth offender you got life.

That's the four-time loser law.

That's right. The result of those mandatory laws was that
everybody was going into prison and nobody was coming out.
And they couldn't build more prisons: a place like Attica would
cost $25, $30 million to build. You know somebody once asked
me: "How do you feel, do you feel that you were a bad guy or
good guy or what?" Well, I think the good I've done in life sort of
balances out my depredation and the money that I stole, because I
used a lot of that money for good purposes. And the result is,
even today, I talk before boys' clubs to dissuade them from a life
of crime.

What did you use the money for?

Huh?

The good purposes. What good purposes?

Well I helped a lot of people out. In fact, I saved five or six
people from going to prison. People that needed money that were
working for farms, and once for an insurance broker. He was living over his head. He came to me one time, and said: "Willie, I
need $10,000 or I'm going to prison." So he told me he had used
this money up which wasn't his, so I gave him the money. And a
manager of a shoe store used someone else's money and he had
taken out all the loans that he could possibly take and I was his
last resort. I gave him money, too.

*What was your attitude about money then. Was it really to
acquire a lot of money, or money to just survive on, or was it to
make the big score and retire?*

Over my long career, my motives changed. In the beginning, I
came from a poor family and in a very tough neighborhood.

Brooklyn.

Brooklyn, that's right. I wanted to do a lot of things for my
people. My people were very religious and when I tried to do
something for them, they refused to take the money. In fact
when I sent some money, they turned it over to a church. So
there was my boyhood dream shattered right there. I knew that I

could never buy them, even if I had honest money, they would believe that I stole it anyway. Then I eloped with a kid that had a lot of money, $16,000. I was about 17.

This was money you took from the safe of the girl's father? Her father's money?

That's right.   And I thought about what money could do. Then I wanted money for what it could buy. I used to buy the best of everything, go to the best places, the fashionable hotels, racetracks. I played along Broadway a lot. First nights and all that. That led me to being called "the Actor." But later on, after the first time when this bastard put me in I think for about 15 jobs, which I always denied. I was always innocent. They started knowing my operandi. Before that they didn't know what was happening. Nobody had ever done anything like this before. They didn't know where to look.

This is later on in your career?

Later on in my career, I was trying to buy a pardon. But I was owed so much time, and I had known people that did buy pardons. In prison.

You mean pay off somebody?

Pay it off, that's right. Sure, you might as well look at the horses right in the face, because it's done and that's it.

Is it still done, do you think?

I think so. Many places it is, but I don't say every place. That became a futile pursuit because no politician would handle me I was publicized so much. I was exploited by every court and every judge, every lawyer, everybody had their own ambitions. They advanced them. So naturally—

You put Willie Sutton away, you go up an inch?

That's right. Every D.A. wants to become governor and every county court judge wants to become a Supreme Court judge. And every lawyer wants to make money.

Let me ask you about the prison escapes. Did you have in your mind a method right from the beginning? You say it was the first thing that entered your mind the first day in prison, escape. Did you have in your mind a concept of tunneling, of getting over

*the wall, or were you just going to play it by ear and look for the
weakness in each prison?*

When I got in prison, I had a look, observed everything. I had
to get the atmosphere of the prison like Sing Sing, for instance; it's
not easy to get out of a maximum security prison like that. I beat
three of them. And nobody would have given me a plugged nickel
for my chances of getting out, but I did. And I think that's one of
the messages in my lectures. To never give up. I have a lot of
determination, a lot of perseverance, a lot of willpower. And I
knew from the very beginning I stepped into these prisons, that I
was going to get out somehow. Naturally I was putting my life on
the line maybe to do it. But I was willing to do that. I would go
on and look for the weak spot, whether it was over the wall, or
under the wall, or whether it was through the front door, however
it was. I would case everything and would get every little piece of
information I could, from people that I could trust in prison. I
would get it all and sort it out and figure out the best chance I
had. That happened in all the three prisons I was in.

Your first break was from Sing Sing?

Yes. When I got to Sing Sing they had brand new cellblocks.
And they used a little psychology on you. They told you that
these bars couldn't be cut and everybody believed it. The authorities circulated this thing. I didn't go for it. I had to try them out.
I did try them and I found out I could cut the bars. That was the
first step in the long series of steps. I had to go through seven
doors.

What did you cut the bars with?

I cut them with a hacksaw.

Where did you get that?

You don't get that. It's not like outside where you want a
hacksaw you go to the hardware store and buy it. That has to
come from some place in the prison, say a plumbing shop, or some
place like that, and it's not easy, because all these things are
checked and doublechecked. Maybe a substitute has to be put
there in its place or something and it takes a little time. But time
—patience— means a whole lot. Stealing today—the thieves don't
have any patience. They want to hit and grab and run. If you tell

somebody this is going to take two or three or four weeks of casing, they don't even want to listen to you. They just want money in a hurry and this here drug situation is the most serious thing we have in the country today, I think. When I was in prison, I met a lot of drug pushers . . . . And boy, I think these people are mass murderers. And I tell you, I might have done a lot of things in my life, robbing banks, but boy, I would think they should put those people up against a wall and shoot them, because I have seen the misery those people cause.

Do you think that capital punishment is a deterrent to murder in the mind of a professional criminal? I'm not talking about the crimes of passion, I'm talking about the professional criminal.

I think in a lot of respects it is a deterrent. I know it was on me as a professional thief.

In other words, you thought in your mind—I won't shoot someone or murder someone because I might go to the chair?

That's right. To me it had that effect. And that's why, I guess, maybe that had some influence on the fact that I never harmed anybody. But a lot of these people—when you meet them in prison—there's an awful large percentage of them who are mentally disturbed people. And I don't think it's a deterrent to them, the electric chair, because they don't think straight in the beginning. When a judge sentences a man for psychiatric treatment to a prison, he is an arch-hypocrite. I'll tell you why. Because there is no psychiatric treatment for an inmate. Why? What psychiatrist would work for a prison, say for $17,000 a year, when he can make $50,000 or $75,000 outside? The result is getting a prison psychiatrist on a part-time basis. Now if you have two or three hundred people in prison you can't give them any kind of real psychiatric treatment on that basis.

We're talking about prison reforms that you feel are needed. Attica, I understand, is a model prison. It's a maximum security prison but it's considered or supposedly considered to be a modern institution.

That's very debatable. Most of the officers, the correctional officers, at Attica, and I think you'll find this true in many prisons, they don't have the qualification to be correctional officers. They lack understanding. They don't understand people. A lot of them came from farms, for instance. They would come in and they would put a guard's uniform on them and it was a case of patrolling and so forth but when it came to understanding people and preventing trouble, they weren't capable of doing that. They always had a defensive mechanism working. They had to be tough. They had to be tough and show these fellas they can't be taken advantage of. I understand that they now have a lot of schools training these people as officers. And that's one of the things that's going to bring dividends to the state and also to the taxpayer.

Why was Arnold Schuster killed? What do you think in your own mind? How did that come about? Schuster being the one who picked you out, on the subway I believe, and identified you and this led to your arrest?

Well, let me put a little thing before that. I have often given that an awful lot of thought. Here's a man that was born 40 years after me and yet his path crossed mine. And it was strictly by chance. I ran and I got on a subway train that I should have missed. And I got on that subway train and he happened to be shopping that day in a business district of Brooklyn and when my train reached the DeKalb Avenue Station, he got on. And it was only a three-minute run from DeKalb Avenue to Pacific Street. And in that time, he made me.

Identified you.

Yeah. Now, this person could never harm me after he identified me. He couldn't testify in my case or anything like that. I was wanted for a two-year-old robbery. He had known nothing about it. And he had absolutely nothing whatsoever to do with me. He could never harm me. And, in fact, it's a pretty lonely life. You get tired of running and the more intelligence you have the more you realize that the day is going to come when they're going to get you. Schuster was a very handsome kid. He had been in the Coast Guard and he had a book with a lot of addresses. And that might have had something to do with it. A person could have, prior to my being arrested and identified by him, prior to that somebody might have wanted to kill him and this was the opportune time to do it. After he identified me. That had nothing to do with me. It might have been something that he himself did—

So you're saying that the possibility existed that someone wanted to kill him and used the opportunity of his identifying you to shroud or to cover his own motives?

That's right.

What about the story of Albert Anastasia, who was the Lord High Executioner of the Mafia in New York City, then watching television and seeing Schuster being interviewed and then going into a fit and saying "I can't stand squealers! Hit that guy!" And Schuster being murdered by one of Anastasia's henchmen, a fellow, ironically, as the story goes, who broke out of prison with you once.

No, I don't buy that, but I would say this—it's a very strong probability that that could have happened. Now I don't know how much faith they could have put in this Valachi. I don't know how much he told them that was true. He must have known a lot of information about them . . . and how much was false or how much was guesswork or speculation. But he was the one that advanced this about Anastasia. And Anastasia was really a crazy person. Now the whole thing is, what gives me a moment of hesitation and refuting something like that, is this. While I was in Attica, the FBI came down to see me. You know? So they told me, that they had closed the books on Freddie [Frederick Tenuto, the Anastasia henchman accused of killing Schuster], which meant that he was dead. The city of New York spent more money investigating that murder than any murder they ever had.

Fred Tenuto, of course, was the fellow you broke out of prison with.

That's right, but you see, in breaking out of prison, you used the people that wanted to get out of prison. I never associated with him within the prison. But he was one of those that wanted to get out. I never saw him from the moment I got over the wall with him.

Do you think he might have shot Schuster and thought he might be doing you a favor?

No, I don't think so. He was known as the Accommodation
Murderer, you know. He was convicted in Philadelphia for killing
two people because some friend of his told him that these guys
harmed him in some way. So, to accommodate his friend, he went
out and killed these two people. But I don't believe that he would
have believed that this man [Schuster] could hurt me in any way.
There would be no motive for him to try to silence him. This was
a three-pronged investigation. There was an investigation by the
government, there was investigation by the state, and an investigation by the city. Now this investigation took them all over—Australia, Europe and elsewhere. Now before I got out, you can bet
that they investigated thoroughly. One of the people that helped
to get me out [of Attica] was the Chief Probation Officer for
Queens County; he had been 25 years in the service. And he
spoke to everybody that was involved in that Schuster case as an
investigator. I was exonerated completely. There was a bookmaker right in Schuster's neighborhood, and he disappeared the
night after Schuster got killed. They never found any trace of this
guy.

You think there might be some connection?

Oh, there must be some connection. He's a bookmaker, known
bookmaker in the neighborhood. And you know, bookmakers are
all connected up and they don't allow you to work in the family
of a bookmaker. He was supposed to be associated with those
guns that were stolen off the docks. See there was a crate of guns
being shipped to Japan, and somebody stole them. Well they
rounded up all of those stevedores and they said that they sold
these guns to the bookmaker and one of the guns was found close
by to where Schuster was murdered.

*Of all the roles and the crimes we're talking about—we're talk-
ing about a hundred banks robbed—is the Schuster murder the
most haunting aspect of your entire criminal career?*

Yes.

Haunts you to this day?

That's true. There must be some kind of a conclusion to this
case, one way or another. They had very good clues. But nothing
comes out. You don't hear anything.

William Faulkner/
One of His Own People

A sullen and brooding man to his death on July 6, 1962, William Faulkner won the Nobel Award (1949) and Pulitzer prizes for his exceptional works of fiction. Faulkner was the first major American author in the twentieth century who devoted the whole of his writings to a particular region in the United States—the South—innovating a style marked by distorted syntax and endless sentences, a structure designed to best fit the thoughts of his unforgettable backwater characters. He proved himself to be a master of dialect who concentrated upon universal problems of evil in the break-up of the family and the degeneration of human character.

Almost all of his works are considered classics today—*The Sound and the Fury, As I Lay Dying, Light in August, Intruder in the Dust, A Fable*—yet Faulkner barely made a living as a writer. He was constantly broke and begging his publishers for money. He drank heavily; some claimed he was an alcoholic. Yet he continued to produce his secular masterpieces, and even did writing stints in Hollywood to support himself (his most important screen credit was *The Big Sleep*, produced in 1946).

Seventeen books—novels, stories and poems—were produced by Faulkner from 1929 to 1944. However at the end of that period, nothing of Faulkner's work remained in print and he was considered "finished" by most critics. Malcolm Cowley, that ingenious literary historian, gathered Faulkner's works, mostly from used bookstores, and studied the Southern writer for months, afterward writing several important critiques of his work. The critic then edited *The Portable Faulkner*, a marvelously balanced collection of the writer's works. In so doing, Cowley single-handedly established William Faulkner as a major author, and is responsible for the Faulkner classics available today.

When success and money did come to William Faulkner, the author gave it a cynical smirk. He made little effort to hide the deep resentment he felt at being ignored for almost two decades. Prior to Cowley's exposition of his work, Faulkner wrote to the critic: "It is my ambition to be, as a private individual, abolished and voided from history, leaving it markless, no refuse save the printed books."

Even after history stamped him a genius, Faulkner continued to "hide out" in his ancestral home in Oxford, Mississippi. He seldom spoke to his neighbors and, when he did, it was either a grunt or a snarl. He shunned outsiders. His drinking increased and probably killed him in the end. And that seemed to matter little to him. He left his "printed books."

Faulkner had few real friends in life and, perhaps, the closest person to him was his brother Dean Swift Faulkner, who died in 1935. The death of the younger brother caused Faulkner to descend into almost permanent gloom, a dark despair that possessed him for years. And, ironically, his brother's fate could have been his own at the toss of a coin.

This was a chapter in Faulkner's life that remained shrouded in mystery, the actual events surrounding the death of his brother never before explained until an inadvertent

Sculptured bust of Faulkner by Leon Khoury, completed during the author's lifetime but not unveiled until William Faulkner Day in 1964 after the writer's death.

conversation with a Chicago cab driver came about in April 1967, the cabbie an eyewitness to an event that produced an instant transformation of William Faulkner from happy-go-lucky barnstorming pilot to morose literary chronicler with a decidedly suicidal bent.

My account of my meeting with the cab driver, one Lowell McSwain, appeared in *Omnibus Magazine* in May 1967, and, in tribute to Faulkner, is written in the dialect as it was spoken by one of his own people, McSwain, who knew Faulkner and his brother Dean Swift during the brothers' barnstorming days in the early Thirties. William Faulkner had served with the British Royal Air Force as a pilot during World War I, and continued his romance with the air as a stunt flier and barnstormer until the traumatic event of his brother's death.

The legions of Faulkner followers might assume that Dean Faulkner's death figures prominently in Faulkner's memorable *Pylon,* his saga of the disillusioned WWI ace, who dies tragically at book's end. This is not the case. *Pylon* was published in March 1935, and Dean Swift Faulkner, with his brother looking on, was killed before stunned spectators in Tupelo, Mississippi, November 10, 1935, strangely foreshadowed, however, by the fate of *Pylon*'s hero.

"Ah got trouble with mah teeth."

At the next red light on Michigan Avenue, the cabdriver turned and smiled, displaying a great oral cavity punctured by only three lower teeth.

"It's awfully hard fo' me ta eat. Yo' caught me comin' outah mah favorite rest'rant. A lil' ol' gal in thyar knows right what ah lyke ta eat." He snorted a laugh. "Ah guess it's gotta be kinda soupy, though."

The day was dull, flat, and overcast. Pedestrians were struggling up the stairs of the Art Institute to view a Manet exhibit.

"What part of the South are you from?"

The cabdriver heaved immense shoulders. "Mississippi. Guess you' knowed by mah accent."

Critic Malcolm Cowley who single-handedly brought about the Faulkner renaissance.

"Yes, I guess so."

From beneath the filmy plastic card on the dash, the driver's face loomed out, florid and grim. *"Your Driver's Name is: LOW-ELL McSWAIN"* the card informed. The card was topped with a Chicago, Illinois, seal.

"What part of Mississippi?"

"You' wouldn't know it, mos' lykely. Small farmin' town. A place called Oxford."

"Oxford?"   Oxford-Faulkner, William Faulkner-Nobel Prize for Literature—*Soldier's Pay, Sartoris, Sanctuary, Pylon.*

I leaned forward. "Did you know William Faulkner, the novelist?" I said.

The cab came to a halt in front of the Palmolive Building (later the Playboy Building). McSwain stopped the meter. "Ah don't know no William Faulkner. Ah knew a Bill Faulkner. Ah knew Bill 'n' Dean, the Faulkner boys."

"Dean?"

"Bill's kid brothah, Dean Faulkner."

"So you knew them both?" I had my hand on the door handle but it would not move.

Lowell McSwain turned almost completely around in his seat to face me, his great jaw bristling with beard stubble. "Yes, ah did, but, hell, tha' were back inna 'Thirtahs. Le's see, nineteen six-teeesevon . . . ah'm fordeee-sevon . . . so ah mus'a bin 'bou' fifteen when it happen' . . . ."

"What do you mean?"

McSwain squinted. "Well, inna 'Thirtahs, ah was a kid livin' in Oxford. Them Faulkner boys was thyar, too. Kinda wild, them. Drinkin' 'n' rasin' the devil. Thyar was another brothah, John, ah guess his name was, but ah didn' see much a' him. Anyway, Bill 'n' Dean Faulkner, they had this crazee lil' air-e-o-plane. Ah guess they called it 'Casino.' Ah think tha's wha' they called it." (William Faulkner and his brother, Dean Swift Faulkner, barnstormed in their plane, *Waco*, throughout the southlands in the early 1930s).

"Did it have one set of wings or two?"

"Two, yes, ah remembah, 'cause ah stood ona wing to get inna tha' crazee plane." McSwain flipped on his turn signal and the heavy Michigan Avenue traffic went around the parked cab.

"Why did you do that?"

"You' mean stan' onna wing?"

"Yes."

"Ah worked for them boys outa a place Bill Faulkner called 'Market Airport.' Hell, weren' no airport, really, a big open fiel' outside a Oxford whyar them boys kept thyar plane. Ah got 50c sometimes a pullin' thyar prop . . . Ol'-fashioned thing, had a pull it 'roun' ta get the crate goin' . . . ."

"Keep talking."

"Them boys were a lotta fun. Bill would wear them high boots an' tha' funnee flyah's cap. Real gentry. They raise all kinsahell, jus' lyke the res' a' us, but they was gentry down in ol' Oxford. Ah wen' outta tha' fiel', now, ah remembah—it was inna yeah nineteen-thirtah-five. 'N' ah got tha' prop-turnin' job on Sundays when them boys were out thyar with tha' ol' plane—actin' lyke it was a human bein', or somethin', fussin' 'n' patchin' her wings, 'n' tinkerin' with her ol' motah." McSwain's face seemed dark with the past, way back there on that pot-holed, grassy field outside of Oxford, Mississippi in 1935.

"Ah saw, the firs' time in mah life, ah saw a woman smokin' in public out thyar. She were a pretty woman, elegan' you' might say. Kinda lyke them flappahs, huh? Dunno who she was, nevah saw her but tha' once, when she was standin' agains' the wing a Bill's plane 'n' Bill was standin' thyar talkin' with her 'n' out she pulled a cigarette 'n' lit ryght up, 'n' mah mouth fell open. 'Loogy, loogy, loogy,' ah yelled, 'n' Bill said, 'Don' point, boy, don' point' 'n' he put mah arm down. Ah guess he thought ah was kinda stoopid. Then, Bill 'n' Dean got inna plane an' ah propped 'em good.

"They took tha' ol' plane 'cross the fiel' an' we all stood back 'n' watched it bounce 'n' jump inna holes, aprayin' tha' they'd get ovah ol' man Gilgore's fence."

"Who was Gilgore?"

McSwain laughed deep and long. "Haaaaa! Ol' man Gilgore! He wore a farmah, owned a corn patch onna othah side o' Bill's

Market Airport 'n' he hated them Faulkner boys. He use' ta come ryght up ta tha' fence 'n' hollah 'n' fuss with a pitchfork or somethin', 'n' scream tha' he was gonna jam in tha' pitchfork in ta tha' lil' ol' plane if they evah touched one shred o' his corn. Ol' Gilgore! He woulda done it, too. Well them boys al'ays made tha' lil' crate jus' fly ryght ovah his fiel', almos' touchin' the top o' them cornstalks 'n' they laughed at Gilgore 'n' laughed, 'n' Bill tried ta bean ol' Gilgore with a bottle once, dropped it ryght down on 'em."

"And what happened in 1935?"

"Huh?"

"You said, 'it happened.' "

"Yes, ah did. It started ta happen when Bill 'n' Dean come flyin' ovah ta Tupulo 'n' they dropped leaflets, lil' papah flyahs tha' tol' evrabodee tha' thyar was gonna be a big air show ovah Tupulo nex' Sunday 'n' they was all ta be thyar ta see the big show. Hell, weren' no big air show, jus' them two Faulkner boys 'n' tha' ol' crate o' thyar's.

"Ah went ovah thyar to Tupulo with them boys nex' Sunday 'n' ah was suprised ta see them Tupulo folks turn out, mos'ly come ta see them air shows in them days, farmahs."

"How did the Faulkners like it?"

"Fine, fine. They fooled aroun' a lot, showin' off the ol' crate lyke it were the greates' thing ta come in ta the air. Bill 'n' Dean did it fo' monee, you' know—two bucks a head. But when they went ta get them folks up in a air, them farmahs didn' want no part o' it. Then Bill talked three farmahs ta go up thyar with 'em. Bill 'n' Dean flipped a coin ta see who was gonna tyake them up. 'N' Dean won. He took 'em up all ryght an' he looped them farmahs 'round' 'n' 'roun', highah 'n' highah, fastah 'n' fastah, an then . . . the damn wing . . . the damn ol' crate . . . the damn ol' wing come ryght off 'n' the plane come down inna crazee-est way ah evah seen. It come all the way down 'n' crashed 'n' them ol' farmahs 'n' Dean were all ovah the fiel' in Tupulo.

"Bill jus' stood thyar sayin' nothin' 'n' watchin' whyar the plane crashed 'cross the fiel', an' then he walked ovah thyar an' he was yellin' inna kinda language ah nevah heard afore, some funnee

Sketch of Faulkner—by an unknown artist—in his British Royal Air Force uniform, 1918; the artist facetiously dubbed in "Pilot."

language, cryin' between the words. Ah saw 'em drink down a whol' bottle o' whiskey . . . ah ain' nevah seen a man do tha' in mah whole life . . . 'n' then he got a sheet or somethin' an' walked all ovah tha' fiel' a pickin' up his brothah 'n' he loaded 'em inna car. Ah asked him, him sittin' inna car sayin' nothin' if ah could go along with him 'n' all he said ta me was, 'No, boy, ah want ta be alone' . . . . Ah nevah seen 'em at the ol' Market Airport agin.

"Ah guess Bill was a hero inna Firs' War 'n' yo' think he'da know 'bou' flyahs dyin' . . ." McSwain stopped and thought about it. "He were a small man, Bill, with keen lil' face, 'n' with ah, 'n' with ah . . . ." McSwain spread two fingers in opposite directions down the edge of his lips. "With ah lil' white mustache 'n' a head o' whyte hyar . . . 'n' busy . . . al'ays scurrin' 'roun' . . . he nevah scurried aftah Dean got killed, 'n' ah nevah saw 'em do nothin' in town, 'cept buy a lota booze at the sto're. 'N' he nevah went out ta Market Airport, not tha' any o' us seen. Maybe he went out thyar when nobodee could see, ah dunno , . . he got strange."

McSwain finally looked at the meter. "Ah guess tha's all ah know 'bout Bill Faulkner, mistah."

I paid him his money. "Ever read any of Faulkner's books?"

"Nooooo, no ah ain' read no books by Bill Faulkner 'n' ah ain' been back ta Oxford since, nineteen-sixtee, ah guess. Befo' tha' it was nineteen-fortee-one. Tha's when ah went inna armee."

I started to step out of the cab.

He pushed one lip into another indifferently. "Faulkner's books any good?" he said half-heartedly.

"Extremely good."

"Maybe ah'll read one some day."

I closed the door and Yellow Cab Driver 7126, Lowell McSwain, pulled into heavy traffic.

Some Faulkner Memorabilia: Faulkner despised Hollywood, though he derived a great deal of money from his screenwriting chores; he was known in filmdom as a "fixer," coming in to rewrite weak scripts, the kind of assignment he preferred over writing original full-length film scenarios. When taking on original screenplay work Faulkner fumed and fussed, hating to write at studio

offices. When working on *The Big Sleep*, Faulkner went to pro-
ducer-director Howard Hawks, asking him if he "could write at
home."

The writer said that he could not produce properly in the hec-
tic studio atmosphere. Responded the kindly Hawks: "Certainly.
Go home, Bill, and write there, if you find that way easier to get
the job done."

Later, Hawks called Faulkner at his Hollywood apartment to
check on the progress with the script. The producer was informed
that Faulkner was not there, but had gone "home" to write . . . all
the way back to Oxford, Mississippi.

One of Faulkner's closest companions, J. Aubrey Seay, recalled
a pensive and modest-to-death writer: "He didn't like to talk about
his writing, or to be talked to about his success. About the time
of the Nobel Award, I saw him coming down the street [in Oxford,
Miss.] and a lady meeting him. I opened the door and watched so
I could hear what they were saying, and I heard her saying, 'How
proud we are! How proud we are!' If he said anything, I didn't
hear it. He just kept walking . . . ."

One legend recalled Ernest Hemingway, so exuberant over the
acceptance of his first published story, "Crucifixion," that he felt
compelled to visit in 1921 the editor who had taken the piece (for
the old *Double Dealer* magazine located in New Orleans). As he
entered the editor's offices, he overheard a little, wiry man with a
thin mustache leaning heavily over the editor's shoulder and telling him that the story was "inane and stupid," vociferously urging
him not to publish it. The little man was William Faulkner, who
had also been recently accepted by the magazine. Hemingway
promptly fell into arguing with Faulkner, and chest surging with
anger, knocked him to the floor. Little Faulkner (he stood about
5'2") immediately jumped up, threw Hemingway to the floor with
an expert wrestling hold, and pinned him until the novelist ceased
arguing. (Hemingway always had bad luck picking fights. Morley
Callahan outpunched him in Paris in 1928. Max Eastman again
wrestled him to a standstill in 1937.) Faulkner thought the whole
thing extremely funny.

Faulkner drawing (signed "Falkner"), reproduced from the 1920-21 *Ole Miss.*

Another story has Ernest Hemingway traveling into Mississippi in the late Twenties to see the Southern novelist "for certain reasons." Taking a room, Hemingway put his young son (his sole companion) to bed "then stayed up all night with a gun on the table waiting for those goons Faulkner writes about to show up," as Hemingway reported to his editor Max Perkins. No one showed up, including the Southern menace, Faulkner.

Once, at a graduate seminar in the steamy southlands, Faulkner was asked to appraise the greatest writers of the twentieth century. He "modestly" complied by listing Thomas Wolfe first, himself second, and many others after, Hemingway being considerably down on the list. When asked why he had placed Wolfe before himself, he said, "Because Wolfe has made the grandest failure!"

Ben Hecht
A Writer for All Seasons

The author first met Ben Hecht in a New York bar in
1958. He was wearing a polka-dot bow tie, a double-breasted
suit and a slouch hat. The rest of the world at the time wore
single-breasted suits and thin, scrawny ties. When I introduced myself to him, he asked: "How did you recognize me?"
I replied: "It was that thin, little mustache."

There was no one like Ben Hecht in American letters, in
journalism, in playwriting, in film dramatizations; he was an
original and reveled in the thought of it. And, unlike most
successful authors I have met, he didn't have a jealous bone
in his creative body.

Hecht's story is well-known, from "picture-chaser" for
the Chicago newspapers in 1911 to star police reporter for
the Chicago *Journal* and then the Chicago *Daily News*, then
to novels, *Erick Dorn* (a minor masterpiece, based upon the
life of the great editor Henry Justin Smith), *Count Bruga,
Broken Necks*, and a host of short stories. Then there were

Ben Hecht: "The policy of my paper was to attack everything."

his plays, chiefly with journalistic side-kick Charles Mac-
Arthur, the unforgettable *Front Page* and the hilarious *Twentieth Century.*

As a literary force, Hecht was a brilliant original, a man
who tub-thumped a whole literary renaissance, Chicago's so-
called renaissance (1912-20), into existence, not only pro-
moting such periodicals as *The Little Review* and *Poetry* but
finding jobs for such poetic lights as Carl Sandburg and Max
Bodenheim, encouraging their writings, and even finding them
publishers. He established public readings and debates; he
founded artistic movements (and discarded them when they
grew boring). It is curious to think what Chicago would have
produced during those halcyon years—or worse, the number
of fine poets and writers who might never have emerged from
the editorial backwaters—without his presence.

Hecht's long career, one that spanned almost forty years,
finished inside the motion picture industry. He was not only
the most prolific screenplay writer in the medium but the
highest paid in its history, producing such Hitchcock classics
as *Notorious* and *Spellbound,* and, along with MacArthur,
action gems such as *Gunga Din, Barbary Coast* and many
others. He also produced and directed such memorable pictures as *Crime Without Passion* and *The Scoundrel.* It was
Ben Hecht who wrote the first major crime picture, *Underworld*, for Josef von Sternberg in 1927. One career Hecht
treasured most was his brief stint as a publisher, from 1923
to 1925, during his last days in Chicago, when he produced
his own irascible newspaper, the Chicago *Literary Times*, an
iconoclastic publication that slaughtered every sacred cow in
sight. "The policy of my paper was to attack everything,"
Hecht proudly stated.

He also encouraged me, after our first meeting, to revive
the publication and, from 1961 to 1970, I busied myself with
that task, in addition to earning a living as a writer-editor. We
produced a newspaper of the fine arts which strove mightily
to bring the New York literati to its knees, which it did not
(but we had fun anyway).

The following interview with Ben Hecht took place in October 1962 at Chicago's Sheraton Hotel (now the Radisson), appearing in the November 1962 issue of *Literary Times*. Hecht, who died April 18, 1964, at age 70, was, at the time of this interview, assigned to cover the scheduled championship fight between Sonny Liston and Floyd Patterson which was to take place later that evening.

As I entered his 23rd-floor suite, I found Hecht sitting on a couch, slippers curling upward from crossed feet, a gigantic cigar extending from a jutting chin. He had been reading a copy of *McCall's Magazine*. Our conversation, quite naturally, centered upon the *Literary Times,* his of almost 40 years earlier and mine, which I had been publishing for less than a year.

You bring copies of the new *Chicago Literary Times*?
Yes. Nothing like yours used to be. [Copies of various issues were spread out on a chair. Hecht thumbed through some of them.]
Sure got the ads. Who gets all these ads?
I do.
That was my big trouble. Getting ads. I used to have one big backer, though. Bob Hertz. Owned a big fleet of yellow cabs then. He liked the idea of the paper and bought a $500 ad in every issue. But see here, let me give you some advice—
Did you ever take any advice when you were my age?
No.
In town for the fight?
Covering it for a New Jersey newspaper. I'm not feeling too well, though. Might not go.
How can you cover the fight?
[Smiling] I've written two stories. [Hecht went to a bureau and pulled open two small drawers at the top, withdrawing two thick manuscripts which he flipped in the air—there were large gaps in the typescript.] Patterson wins in this story. [He held it up.] Liston wins in this one. [He held the other manuscript aloft.]

But how do you know who'll win?

[Hecht slipped the stories back into the bureau, smiling and puffing on his cigar.]   In about an hour I'm going upstairs [to another floor] and meet some of the old boys—Buddy McHugh and some others.   [Newsmen from Hecht's era; McHugh in fact was portrayed by his own name in *The Front Page*.] We're gonna play poker. There's a radio up there and I'll listen to the fight and fill in what's necessary for the stories. You play poker? You can sit in.

Not your kind of table stakes. [I have always regretted not sitting in on that poker game.]

Do you have decent copywriters for the paper?

What do you mean?

Good writers, newspaper men and the like. That was my trouble. Getting writers who could make sense without getting esoteric.

They're pretty good. Independent, but good.

Who are they?

Young smart-alecks, like me. But you had a lot of help in the Twenties, didn't you?

Not much.

What about Bodenheim?

[Looking out the window] He was in New York. He wrote from New York then.

And Hemingway was gone from Chicago by then, too?

He was never part of the bunch. I think he left to go to work in Paris for the *Toronto Star* by the time I was putting out my paper.

How did you get along with him when he did live in Chicago? I believe he edited a trade magazine then, just after World War I.

Something like that. Hemingway was not a likeable fellow. Too much concerned with his own *art* [Hecht dragged out the word with a little grimace], and not enough with living. I invited him once to have lunch with the boys but he never showed up. We weren't his kind of people, I guess. He was an *artist*; we were newspaper bums. The only one of us he bothered with was Swatty [Hecht's nickname for Sherwood Anderson, who had read some of Hemingway's early fiction and encouraged him to go on writing]. You would see him with Swatty sometimes. He kept to himself. He waved whenever I saw him but that was it. It seemed to me as if he couldn't wait to get the hell out of Chicago.

How about MacArthur?

He was gone by then, long-gone from Chicago. In fact I was alone. Most of the crowd had moved off by then. [Looking up from his gaze at the churning lake] What's this Old Town? [A section of Chicago which enjoyed, during the 1960s, a reputation as an "artistic" center.]

Wells Street, North Avenue and further up.

To Fullerton?

Around there.

Yeah, I know the area. Bunch of artist bums used to hang up there.

They still do.

I used to be up there, too. The whole bunch of us.

Sherwood Anderson?

Him, Sandburg, Lewis [Lloyd Lewis, the Chicago historian], everyone. Hemingway, too.

What was he doing then?

Writing for some catalog publication. I can't remember what. He had just been married. He was the editor of a magazine. We were impressed.

What about our literary situation today?

What literary situation?

Compared to the days of the Little Review.

Margaret Anderson. We never knew when she'd get that magazine out. She had an amazing way of avoiding creditors. She hid under desks, in closets, everywhere. Most of the time she charmed them. Today [tossing *McCalls* out the window], garbage. Nothing around today but garbage. For a few years there was some good stuff. Then came seven or eight years when books of how to screw were published and everything cheapened. There aren't any markets anymore for the really good writers. The markets are all gone. [He stood up and fixed his eye once again on the lake and said, almost inaudibly, to himself—"Mencken"] But now, all the smart little boys with their nicely-starched white collars have taken over the literary stuff and the arts. They soft-pedal it to everyone who can afford to buy those goofy abstracts or cheap, stupid novels. Watch. It'll get worse, too.

What do you mean?

It'll get so that everybody is just as good as everybody else.

Like who?

Aww, like anybody—what do you want? Names? Trying to get me to blast off, huh?

Why not?

Yeah, it's a lot of fun, but not for those getting it.

That's just it. It's fun. Something you like doing and if everything is said just so, without names, without personalities, then there's something dead, something that says nothing about anybody or anything. Those who say personalities don't count in literary or artistic works are crazy . . . avoiding the fact that flesh and blood creates flesh and blood. Agree?

I wrote something like that in *Child of the Century*. In fact, I wrote everything there was to write in that book.

It was a good book. People have been imitating that book ever since you wrote it.

I remember writing about how I interviewed people like Ibañez—stuffed shirts who not only refused to say anything important or exciting but refused to get out of bed to talk to you.

You wrote something about his little toes protruding from the sheets when you interviewed him, didn't you?

No, Charlie did that. MacArthur.

He had a good sense of humor.

A wild one, but that's what these guys around here lack, you see. A sense of humor. Not one of them can take a rib. It's not in them. They're fakes.

Like who?

There you go again. [Smiling] How long you been working the newspapers?

Some years.

Yeah, the newspapers are sort of dead around here now. Not like when I was around. Not like the roundhousers I used to know. These guys nowadays shave too much. Too many pink faces pretending to be interested in the wire services. They go home at five o'clock. Their wives have made them big dinners. They watch television.

Probably some of your old movies?

God!

You know a guy named Herman Kogan? He's trying something new on your old sheet—the News—*a stab at regional culture.* [A literary section, "Panorama," in the Chicago *Daily News*, now defunct.]

Kogan? Kogan? No. I knew a guy named Coogan though. He used to be up at the old *Daily News*. Used to get our coffee down the street. We used to save up change after the binges and throw it in a pot for the coffee and rolls—we lived off that stuff for the week. Coogan came around and got the coffee. One time the bastard hauled off with the entire pot of dough and we starved for a week.

Must have been fun.

Loads of fun.

What about your new book Gaily, Gaily?

Playboy, you mean?

I did like the piece [parts of *Gaily, Gaily* were being serialized in the magazine] *about a black dancer you knew from your reporting days.*

She really lived here in Chicago; all of those people in the new book are based on people I knew—

When you were a newspaperman?

Yes, artists, lovers, killers, crooked politicians—wonderful copy. I suppose you have them still?

You can't run out of them in Chicago, especially the politicians. How do you feel coming back to Chicago like this, a visitor?

The town's changed for sure. [He looked out the window.] It's a different city now but it was always changing when I was here. That's what Chicago's all about—change. It loves change. Christ, it makes you feel like a gypsy! [Hecht went to a small table and poured two drinks of bourbon, handing me one.] There is no literary situation because there are no individuals, mostly.

[He tipped his glass to me, then belted down his drink.]   You know that. [The phone rang and Hecht answered it.]   Already? Everybody's up there now? Good. I'm on my way. [He hung up the phone, scooped up his two articles on the championship fight, walked me to the door, and out into the hallway. We pressed the elevator buttons and waited. I studied the man puffing leisurely on his cigar—a bit Falstaffian, almost completely bald, a bit stooped, but the pencil mustache remained. His movements were still quick and there was fire in his eyes. Two elevators, one headed up and the other down, arrived simultaneously and we stepped inside, looking at each other. Hecht appeared a bit odd, wearing his slippers, filling his elevator with blue smoke from his cigar. He smiled widely and gave a short salute.] Keep it up. I'm in Nyack [New York]. Remember to send the issues of the paper.

    Sure will.

    [He went up and I went down; it was the last time I saw him alive.]

Jasper Johns/
The Art of the Matter

A painter of the physical, the identifiable abstract, as it were, in an era when "pop art" predominated, Jasper Johns, a southerner by birth (Augusta, Georgia, May 15, 1930), became a world-renowned artist since this interview in August 1964. His paintings are now permanently exhibited in New York's Museum of Modern Art, the Tate Gallery in London, in Stockholm, and in Holland.

Johns not only vehemently denied belonging to the Warhol school (or any other school for that matter) but insisted that his work was unique, which it is, and that he was a private creature made public "by the public." A painter of targets, flags, maps, Johns' creativity has always gone beyond the stereotype, which, in his art, he establishes at the beginning before altering, reshaping and then eliminating with his own singular images.

Like most modern and innovative artists, Johns is not easy to explain, nor is he particularly interested in trying to verbalize his work, and, during the course of the interview, the words of William Snaith (from *The Irresponsible Arts*) flitted in my mind before and after Johns' words: ". . . as long as the artist strives for communication, however strange the language or symbol, he has the right to demand that we understand him."

The interview took place in a New York City penthouse, looking down on Riverside Drive, where Johns was then living, and appeared in the September, 1964 issue of *Literary Times*. An elevator with a liveried operator took me up to a single entranceway. A maid answered the door, and showed me into an expansive apartment where the broad walls were white and nothing boasted of opulency. I was led into a large room having a long sofa, one chair, and many new wooden boxes traditionally used to pack peaches. The maid disappeared out onto a balcony. From the windows you could see the Hudson streaming in blue ripples to the sea. The city's morning haze dwelled and puffed below. Johns emerged from a balcony, smiling, with a long piece of wood in his hand. He went directly to the lone chair, sat down, motioned me to the sofa in a friendly manner, and then asked the maid to bring coffee, which she did.

I hear you're leaving for South Carolina in the next week or so. Is this your home?

I try to live there as much as I can but I have to be in New York most of the time. I'm from there [South Carolina] originally. Three or four years ago I got a house down there but then I got a commission to do some work at Lincoln Center, so I had to be here.

Where do you live down there?

I live on Edistoe Island. Except during the resort season, there are only four families living on the island. My place is on the beach . . . 40 miles to the nearest movie.

What effect has being a Southerner had on your work in your opinion?

Well, since I was born there, I don't really know.

Jasper Johns in 1964.

Although you deny being a "pop" artist, you sometimes use such things as beer cans, light bulbs, etc., in your work. Doesn't this seem inconsistent?

No. I don't think of myself as a "pop" artist. Generally, people called the "pop" movement single-minded . . . . It is technically more restrictive and deals mostly with images. I am not so much interested in dealing with images as working for form.

A number of painters—not only the "pop" painters, but people like Rivers and yourself—have concerned themselves with Americana subject matter (maps of the U.S., Confederate flags and soldiers, portraits of George Washington, etc.). Do you think this reflects an increasing nationalistic pride in artists?

I don't think so. I'm merely concerned with looking and seeing and not much else. I'm not involved in patriotism or politics.

Do you feel that a feeling of nostalgia for the Thirties and early Forties is in any way responsible for the emergence of "pop" art?

Well a number of artists—Pollack, Motherwell, de Kooning—drew a great amount of attention to American painting in the Forties. But I don't think this had anything to do with "pop" art. At least, I hope not!

Do you feel that the use of commercial subject matter such as Campbell soup cans, Brillo boxes, etc., reflects an acceptance of or at least a coming to terms with American materialism on the part of American artists?

It is not one of my subjects. Warhol does that sort of thing.

Speaking of Brillo boxes, we understand that the designer of the boxes is upset because of Warhol's use of his exact design. Are there any problems of plagiarism involved here?

In the world of trademarks it is difficult to claim ownership of anything.

In the 1950s were you consciously reacting against "the flood-tide exploitation of abstract expressionism"?

Well, the work I was doing then probably came because of some awareness of what was happening in art. I tried to consciously avoid making statements that were already being made well. The 1940s did something valuable with the work of Pollock and others. In the 1950s there was a hangover where they were not

"Map," 1962 by Jasper Johns. (Weismann Collection)

producing private but painting public pictures and refining statements. I am not interested in refinement. I try to avoid resem-
blances. While I am working on a picture, if it begins to suggest
what someone else has done, I try to work it some other way.

You stated in an interview in Art News *that you are concerned
with a thing not being what it was, but with its becoming something other than what it was. Is this related at all to the double or
ambiguous images of Dali and Tchelitchew?*

I don't identify in such a way, nor am I concerned with that
judgment—good or bad. I don't know what elements enter into it.
Dali? He uses mental images and not visual ones. I know it is difficult to define the difference between the two but it is all tied up
with the Freudian concepts—that kind of juxtaposition.

*Do you feel that today, more than ever, you must promote
your art as a public figure much the same way Picabia and
Duchamp of the Dada Movement did?*

Painters are not public but rather are born in private. The
public has made it their business; however, for the painter, art will
never be public. Of course one man's humor is another's seriousness. For example, Duchamp said, "I must destroy art for myself
so that it will not be destroyed for you." But basically it is not so
much a public action.

*Yes, and Picabia once stood before hundreds at the Champs
Elysee Pavilion and proclaimed, "My friends and I are now painting our paintings offstage and soon we shall sell them to you for a
good deal of money." And he did, and so did they. Now, honest-
ly, don't these Dadaistic gimmicks do the same for you?*

They were pranksters.

*You seem to feel that the observer of a work of art acts in
some way as an artist himself when he views and interprets a work.
Do you feel that the purchaser of a work of art has the right to
alter an artist's original product?*

Well . . .

*For instance, a sculptor recently sold a work entitled "New
Love on an Old Mattress." This work pictured a couple involved
in whatever couples do on mattresses and the mattress was an old,
seedy, flea-ridden object. A wealthy person living in Chicago's*

North Shore area purchased the work, but when displaying it found the bug-infested mattress too repulsive and replaced it with a Sealy-Posture-Pedic or something. When the sculptor visited his work he hit the ceiling and accused the person of destroying his masterpiece. Do you think she had the right to change the work?

She did not have the right. Nevertheless, there may be a time when that type of thing will be quite normal. I would guess that the sculptor in question is George Siegal.

What young artists interest you most at this time?

It is difficult for me to pinpoint people that way. Since I don't see enough of a particular young person's work, I am unable to view his production as a unit. I like the work of Frank Stella—a geometrical painter. He's called a stripe painter. I'm also partial to the sculpture of John Chamberlaine and very interested in his work.

[Motioning to a huge edifice of welded metals looming like a black menace from the corner of another room.] *Is that work done by Chamberlaine?*

[Smiling] Yes, it is.

One last question. Do you feel that there is a natural antipathy between writers and painters?

I don't have many for close friends.

Well, I've always found it difficult to talk to painters.

I think that is because a painter talking isn't using his media while a writer talking is using words.

The Nationalization
Of Gwendolyn Brooks

As a poet and novelist (*Maud Martha*), Gwendolyn Brooks has developed an ethnic literature that is wholly and definitively her own. She has, for more than 35 years, chronicled black Chicago, its streets, its people, its ambitions and failures, but most importantly its struggle to work beyond survival to the dignity that achievement brings. Always an eloquent social voice, Gwendolyn Brooks committed herself to the voices of black militants, if not their excesses, in the late 1960s. This was the subject of the profile the author published in *Chicagoland Magazine* in September, 1969.

Gwendolyn Brooks is a big woman, tall and angular. Her broad forehead and prominent jaw are pierced by dark eyes, intent, watching. She sat in her small office in the administrative complex of Teacher's College, where she is an instructor, against a spartan background of white walls, undecided whether to sit in toward her desk or away from it. Though we had known each other for some time, there was an uneasiness, a hesitancy in her

Gwendolyn Brooks after a poetry reading.

manner and inside her throaty voice. She was, unlike all other encounters where warm outpourings of enthusiasm, of reception to strange ideas and new faces had been commonplace in her make-up, on guard.

There were rumors that had preceded the meeting—rumors that were snidely snorted from the lips of Chicago writers: Gwendolyn Brooks? Oh, she's gone over. Gone over to what? To them, you know, the bloody militants, the angry little people with clenched fists. Gwendolyn Brooks! You mean the poet, the soft, the gentle woman with verse spun into her classroom, the woman of communion with white writers and black writers, embodying the *Weltanschauung* of Midwestern literature?

And the rumors were in her restless mood, confronting a whirring tape recorder, a scatter of yellow papers, notes, my tipped and tripping pen. We were friends but Gwendolyn Brooks had something to say that would touch that, too.

Miss Brooks, now in her middle years and married to the quiet Henry Blakely, was an ethnic writer—not ethnic by race or religion, but by neighborhood, the square blocks of familiarity in Chicago. In the beginning, hers was the knowledgeable sidewalk where her race made up the people-at-large rather than archaic Indian apartheids, or castes such as in the deep South had socially created the Creole, octoroon or quadroon.

And her youth was spent in watching the neighborhood people toil through time, and the youth of her writing was a chronology and a lecture "We real cool, we quit school . . . we die young," to those who broke the better human pattern.

Born June 7, 1917, in Topeka, Kansas, Miss Brooks has lived almost all her life in a quiet neighborhood on Chicago's South side. It was not the doom of slums inherited by Richard Wright's Bigger Thomas. Those native sons were rare in her early days. It was quiet enough to see the storms and certain children drifting into the shapes of outcasts. Her literary passion burned slowly and the evolution brought forth in 1945 the poignant *A Street in Bronzeville.* Then honors—two Guggenheim Fellowships, awards from the American Academy of Arts and Letters, the *Mademoi-*

selle and *Poetry* awards.   Her second volume of poetry, *Annie Allen*, won her the Pulitzer Prize in 1949.

But for the white community that ran the literary business then, Gwendolyn Brooks was no threat that might bring about volatile eruptions in American literature.   The status quo would remain and she would do little to change it.   She was not change, but a steady breeze.

Years meshed and Gwendolyn Brooks' stature in American letters, though national, became something exclusively Chicago, like the city's almost puerile pride in the now defunct stockyards.

In 1968, Gwendolyn Brooks was officially named by the Governor as The Poet Laureate of Illinois.

"What does that mean?" Miss Brooks said, opening the interview with a challenge.   "I mean what does one do when one becomes The Poet Laureate of Illinois?   I haven't the slightest idea. It's certainly a nice honor but it's a title I didn't seek.   In fact, with what's been going on, I'm amazed!"

"What do you mean when you say 'with what's been going on'?"

"I mean the social changes happening in Chicago and the people making them happen . . . my people!"

"Your people?"

"Black people."   These words were blurted but as direct and purposeful and expeditious as Travis drawing his sword in line through the dust of the Alamo's square.   No quarter—from Travis, from Santa Anna, from Gwendolyn Brooks.   Sound the *Deguelo*.

"That's the first time I've ever heard you put it that way, that definite and apart.   I thought humanity—all of it—were your people."

"That's the problem, you see," she said and her eyes wandered briefly about the room.   "My young friends, young black writers, have been chastising me for not making a stand for my own race . . . for not saying loud enough that I'm a black writer."

"You're a writer.   I'm a writer.   There are no colors, no shades."

"I don't believe that."

"Anymore?"

"Anymore."

"It sounds like your young friends have been practicing intimidation."

"Oh, no, no, no, no. It's far from that. It's my realization, it's my awareness and it took these young people to make me aware of my responsibility to my race."

"What does that mean?"

"It means that I must participate in the movement, I guess that's what you would call it."

Already, I had been categorized, purely for identification purposes, of course.

"I, Whitey."

"I meant that in a general sense. There are many types of emancipation and we are now living in an age where my people are unsatisfied with society. They are seeking a new emancipation."

"And that is?"

"Oh, you know, you're an intelligent person. It's one of acceptance and of economy, of jobs—not just jobs—of positions and the right to get into those positions by ability and these young people have that ability, that talent."

"They are also extremely militant in their ways of getting those positions. The clenched fist, the implied saber-cut, the rifles and pistols that are loaded . . ."

Gwendolyn Brooks smiled sadly. "Well, they are angry. They have a right to be angry when they've been denied privileges white America enjoys."

"And where do you think this anger will take them . . . or you?"

"They are doing something and they have gotten smart. They write for our race and their writings are read by blacks and blacks publish their words and they don't care if the white man ever reads them, ever publishes them."

"But you know that ever since you and Richard Wright and Langston Hughes and others first appeared, the American public as a whole has accepted you."

"That was different. The time then was different."

"In other words, you were safe."

"I don't quite get your meaning."

Gwendolyn Brooks, the talented Poet Laureate of Illinois.

"As a Negro—"

"Black."

"As a black, you and others were safe, your themes, ideas, were not as incendiary, as, say, someone like LeRoi Jones."

"You mean the period in which I was awarded the Pulitzer Prize? Yes, I guess so; you could say that."

"And what about the Pulitzer? What did you think of at the time, that a Ne—a black woman was awarded such a distinguished prize?"

"I thought it was nice but I was a different person then. We grow. In fact, I receive a lot of criticism from young black writers because I won that prize and didn't do anything about it and they are right."

"What could you have done?"

"I could have been more active to further my people. Naturally winning the prize made me—oh, I don't know—known, I guess. Recognized. I could have used it. But that's all over anyway. We grow inwardly now, work inwardly."

"In other words you don't need the prize for recognition or the Poet Laureate thing."

"Yes."

"But what about the public, your readers to be specific, they aren't all black. I'd say your readers are equally white. Don't you feel you have an obligation, if not to them, then to the talent you have supplied to them?"

"I'm still writing. Lord! I'm working hard at it but it's slow and I'll continue to publish."

"In the white press."

"In the black press whenever I can and if they will accept me."

"But you're a poet, a fine one, not merely a black writer."

"I'm a black woman, let's face it."

"What?"

"When I come into a room, what do you see?"

"Gwendolyn Brooks."

"No, you see a black woman."

"That's not correct. I see Gwendolyn Brooks."

"You don't really see me, you see a black woman, like any

other black woman. That's first, that will always be first. But it's nice of you to say it the other way."

"I'm surprised at you, subscribing to that theory of 'They all look the same.' "

"Well . . . don't we?"

"Not at all."

"You're a writer," she said somewhat disgusted at not getting the point over. "You see things and people a bit differently because you're looking for something. But we are talking about your race seeing my race and that is strictly a black and white thing!" She broke into nervous laughter. Her face mellowed from the consternated look vanguarding her words. It was as if she was remembering something without a name, perhaps an old propriety.

"God! I sound so awful!"

"What kind of contact have you had recently with young black writers?"

"I've attended their college black writers' conferences . . . their workshops . . . classes . . . on the street, and in the home, you might say."

"And what do they say to you?"

"They quite naturally expect me to help them, be part of them . . . and I am. They want nothing to do with the white race. They realize what the white race has done to them, perhaps more than any other black generation realizes it."

"You mean slavery—the old one in the South."

"That's part of it."

"But the blacks in Africa really began slavery among themselves, the coastal tribes raiding the inlands of their own country and selling their own people to the Portuguese, the Dutch, even when the white traders were reluctant to accept such war booty. So it's not strictly the white man's responsibility—the beginning of mass slavery, that is. I'm sure you're aware of that."

"I really didn't know that. Where did you discover that?"

"In books such as *Black Cargoes* written by Malcolm Cowley."

"Malcolm Cowley wrote that?"

"In collaboration with another writer [Daniel P. Mannix]. It is a well-researched book."

"I haven't read that book. I'll have to get it."

"There are others."

"Yes." She thought for a minute, then in her honest sophistry, asked, "What do you think of when you think of the word Negro?"

"When I was young, I thought of Africa—a place on the map— it was strictly a geographical concept most young boys had then, I think, especially when you lived in a small town such as Green Bay, Wisconsin, where I lived and the only time you ever saw a Negro was at the local theater as a side-kick to Charlie Chan who was frightened of the dark and rolled his eyes and got nervous and was funny."

"And what did you think of him, this Negro on the screen?"

"I thought he was imported, I guess, but I was a small boy and had never seen a Negro. It was a small town and there were no Negro ghettos, nothing like that. The cab drivers, the bus drivers, were all white. Later, on trains, I began to see them."

"Yes, and you see that is how white America grew up. No one has ever seen us. We are Americans!"

"Of course. Whites, blacks, all Americans. That still doesn't mean that the black man with intelligence in his head and anger in his heart, has the answer for his race in a clenched fist, does it?"

"All I know is that they must accomplish their work, their goals, on their own. But getting back to what you said about geography. You see that's the trouble, the problem with whites understanding blacks. Their ideas are remote and archaic. They still think of us as Africans, and we are Americans . . . ."

"What about the many blacks who want to go back to Africa, who want all blacks to leave America, or, at least, have certain states turned over to them for exclusive black residency?"

"What would we do in Africa? Africans live in Africa. They were born there, one generation after another. That is not our country. America is our country."

"And yet your young black friends want to divide it, to withdraw the black race from it, to act as a separatist nation within a nation."

"Oh, they don't want that. They want to achieve things within and for the black race. They do not want to live on the white man's terms. They want to create their own terms, ways of life, and when the time comes . . . if it ever comes . . . to face with equality the white man's society with their own. These young black writers and artists and workers are dedicated and talented and they are determined to go their own way."

"Are you going with them?"

Gwendolyn Brooks thought inside silent seconds, weighing her passions, her belief, no doubt.

"Yes," she said. "I am with them."

She is a kind woman with goodness of talent and intention. She is a writer who for over a decade was a comfortable link in letters between black and white, carefully or unknowingly tiptoeing around quicksand issues, confrontations that would lead the white literary community of Chicago to no longer utter patronizingly, "Our gal, Gwen." But no more−. Goodbye, social teas. Goodbye, aesthetic podiums. Goodbye, token awards. Goodbye, fair-skinned writers.

Goodbye, goodbye.

Bud Freeman:
A Jazzman's Jazzman

Urbane, witty, gregarious, Lawrence Bud Freeman presents anything but the stereotyped image of the jazzman as a noncommunicative mumbler who, like Kaspar Hauser, possesses an inner gift he cannot explain. His dapper dress and polished manners are more the characteristics of a British baron than a man who has been playing a tenor sax in clubs, with big bands and at concerts for more than 57 years, a jazz great who looks upon his enormous talent and his immeasurable contribution to the field with no more vanity than a postman remembering yesterday's mail.

At 75, this style-setting innovator walks several miles a day to exercise, voraciously reads newspapers, magazines and books by the score, is an avid motion-picture goer, and, without fail, puts in his hours of practice each day on the saxophone. His conversation is that of the universal scholar, for his acute curiosity has goaded him into all areas of knowledge, esoteric and public, from anthropological theories to understanding the twisted roots of xenophobia. Freeman's obses-

Bud Freeman in Chicago, 1981. (Photo by Cathy Anetsberger)

sion, of course, is people, and as one of the most durable and accomplished jazzmen of our time he has known them—blue-blooded royalty, gangsters, authors, actresses, geniuses and crackpots. And he has a love for humanity that is indefatigable. People, of course, audiences around the world, have been his business and his pleasure all his life.

Freeman's life has been rich with adventure and achievement. Born in Chicago in 1906, Freeman's jazz career began in the early 1920s when he met Jimmy and Dick McPartland at Austin High School. It was here that Freeman also met Frank Teschemacher and Dave North, who were to make up the original "Austin High Gang" jazz band. He began playing a C-Melody sax in 1923 and then, two years later, switched to a tenor sax which he has stayed with through his long and distinguished career.

The Austin High jazz band, after listening to the New Orleans Rhythm Kings, then led by King Oliver and Louis Armstrong, in the early 1920s, developed what has come to be known as the "Chicago Style" of jazz. Freeman joined the Ben Pollack band in 1927 and later played with every major band in the country—Tommy Dorsey, Benny Goodman, Red Nichols, Roger Wolfe Kahn, Eddie Condon, but remained one of the great jazz soloists in the history of the medium. In the words of one jazz critic, Freeman's "playing is marked by a tenacious, joyful approach to the most basic of jazz tenets: swinging. Making excellent use of vibrato, he has a highly personal way of treating ballads—tender, yet without maudlin sentimentality—and his elliptical phrasing and almost deadpan tone are other aspects of his art which help make him the wholly distinctive player he is."

Freeman's solo classics, and there are scores of them, include: "Smoke Gets in Your Eyes," "Who?" "Maple Leaf Rag," "Marie," "After You've Gone," "Beale Street Blues," "The Eel" (his own masterpiece composition from *Home Cooking*, a collector's album), "I'm Beginning to See the Light" and many, many more. Bud Freeman has composed dozens of jazz pieces and has cut more than 500 sides. He has performed in clubs and concerts throughout the United States, South America, and Europe, where he is thought of, and rightly so, as a jazz master.

The following interview took place in Chicago in October 1981 at the Corona Restaurant.

Someone once said that if you're content with yourself and what you do in life, your life will be a long one. Is this true of jazz artists?

It's true for Eubie Blake. About three years ago I was living in Europe, playing a music festival with Eubie, the great Eubie Blake, ragtime piano composer [James Hubert Blake, born 1883, compositions include "I'm Just Wild About Harry" and "Memories of You," among a host of others], and we were staying at the Meridian Hotel. Just around the corner from the Meridian is a big gambling casino. I was in there till about five o'clock in the morning, and I came around to the hotel, having lost money playing roulette, and in the lobby was Eubie Blake, who was then 95 years old. And he was sitting with a lovely girl, sort of 20-ish, and I said, "Eubie, would you mind if I tell your young lady friend how lovely she is?" And he said, "Would I do that to you?" And he was smoking and I said, "Uncle Eubie, what are you doing up at this hour? Smoking?" He said, "Bud, I've been smoking since I was six years old." I believe that. So the people who think that smoking is a dangerous thing should really consult Eubie Blake.

He was on a television program if I remember correctly a couple of years ago, and they asked him "How do you manage to stay so lively at your age, so enthusiastic?" He said, "Well I enjoy life. I enjoy everything in life." He was asked if he had a special diet. He said, "Oh, no, I eat anything I want. I drink anything I want." And the interviewer said: "Do you mean to tell me you drink strong spirits?" He said, "I hate to tell you this, but I drink every kind of known spirit there is and smoke. I'm just awful. I smoke, I drink spirits, and I eat candy by the handfuls."

I had a friend who died a few months ago. He was playing this British club in London. His name was Lennie Felix and he told

me the year that he played Nice, he did a piano duet with Eubie Blake, and they got into this thing—Eubie must have been maybe 93 years old then—and they got into a duet, the two pianos are back to back. And Eubie looked over to Lennie, playing very quick tempo, and said, "Hey man, what are we playing?"

I was at a party in New York once with my brother Arnie [Arnold Freeman, the noted character actor], and Eubie Blake was there. I remember telling Eubie that we had been listening to his recordings from the start, things like "Railroad Blues," which is one of the first great boogie-woogie style piano solos. And Eubie asked us, "How old were you two when you first heard that tune?" And my brother said, "I think we were about six months old." Eubie wrote a great number of Broadway shows. All those years ago he should have been making the kind of money that other composers were making, but he wasn't.

Why not?

The racial thing that existed in those days.

You mean black artists were given a short count on royalties?

I'm not certain how it worked but I do know that Fats Waller used to sell masterpieces for $50.

Outright?

Yes, oh, yes. The racial attitude in those days was absurd. I recall one Broadway show, sponsored, of course, by white people, and Eubie Blake wanted to write a waltz for this show—you know "I'm Just Wild About Harry" was originally written as a waltz— and the man who was investing money in the show said, "Who ever heard of a black man writing a waltz?" And Eubie said, "I did." So it went in.

Black musicians and composers in this country, at the beginning, and we're going back here to Scott Joplin and W. C. Handy, first found their audiences in bordellos, didn't they? They were the fellows downstairs playing the piano?

Absolutely. Jelly Roll Morton [pianist-composer Ferdinand Joseph La Menthe, 1885-1941] was a great friend of mine and he worked in one, told me all about it. You know Brahms and Jelly Roll Morton had really the same kind of background. Brahms wrote all those fantastic pieces in bordellos. Jelly Roll told me

Freeman: "I never wanted to do musically what one has to do to make a lot of money." (Photo by Lauren Deutsch)

that the girls working in the bordellos felt the blues, felt his music deeply.   I doubt very much if the girls working the bordellos in Vienna understood Brahms or dug him very much.   You know I was listening to Studs Turkel play a piece the other day, "Kitten on the Keys" by Zez Confrey, and Studs said that Zez Confrey was influenced by Scott Joplin and I say no.   What I hear in "Kitten on the Keys" was James P. Johnson, from the Morton era [James Price Johnson, born 1891, one of the finest of the so-called "stride" school of piano players, composer of many standards, "If I Could Be With You," "Old-Fashioned Love," "Charleston," "Runnin' Wild"].   He seldom got credit.   James P. Johnson made all those wonderful old piano rolls and never got any credit for that.

The automatic piano rolls?

Yes, such things as you pumped.   James P. Johnson did so many of those, and he was a genius.

The first significant composition of George Antheil, "the bad boy of music," involved piano rolls—"The Ballet Mechanique" had four or five piano rolls going, in addition to myriad noisemakers, going at all times during the performance of that piece, if I remember correctly.

That's right.   George Antheil was a pianist before he became a great composer.   He was playing a series of concerts in Europe, his own way, at that time way-out works, and the audience in Paris booed him so badly that after the intermission, he brought out a pistol and ostentatiously put it on the piano.   Antheil looked out at the audience, as much to say, "I'm ready for you," and finished the concert.   The Parisians were very difficult.   When Stravinsky went to do *The Rite of Spring* they just about exploded.

A difficult way to make a living, which proves what about the adage of the artist suffering in his own time?

Brahms, Beethoven, Liszt—most of the composers of that period did not make the kind of money that composers make today. The large Bach family made a living playing, writing and selling church music, so I think they were pretty solvent.   I don't know that Mozart ever made a lot of money.   Ravel and Stravinsky made a lot of money.   So when you mention something about our time, in your own time, I think the modern composers made it in their own time, especially the modern jazz players. Now Dizzy Gillespie, if I may jump all over the place, was able to sell his music. He made a fortune. Charlie Parker, had he not been ill, would have made it big. Coleman Hawkins made a lot of money.

And you?

I never wanted to do musically what one has to do to make a lot of money. I like the idea of money but I have a little thing that I do [his music], that I've been doing for 57 years, that has become dear to me. It isn't a thing that I find easy to sell, but now I make a living. But getting back to the artist making a living —the days of the garret are gone.

Nobody wants to starve.

Exactly, and besides, garrets now cost $1,000 a month.

There has been a population explosion since 1930 when we had 130 million people in this country. Now we've got 220 million. The increase of the part of the population that always sponsored the artists, and I do include music, of course jazz, has got to be large enough now so that it can enrich these artists where prior to that there just weren't enough people to properly support them.

Here is the United States, considered to be the richest country of this world, but it doesn't seem to know that the only art form it has—really an art form—is jazz music. Doesn't it seem incredible that all the famous jazz people go to Europe to play their thing, because when they're here they don't play just jazz, they have to play commercial things? They're always in Europe. I found that I had to go to Europe. I was surprised to find how well known I was in Europe. Let us take a jazz artist who is nearly known here. Nearly, you know. Not famous, but known; he is famous in Europe. People recognize him in the street.

I think the American jazz enthusiast really doesn't realize the enormous support that jazz artists, especially from this country, receive in a country like Germany.

There are 200 jazz clubs in Germany. Two hundred!

Solely devoted to jazz?

Yes.

Early 1920s photo of Benny Goodman, Jimmy McPartland and Bud Freeman (top). The band that first influenced Bud Freeman and the Austin High Gang, King Oliver's Creole Jazz Band, circa 1920. Oliver is standing at left, Louis Armstrong is seated third from left (bottom).

Are they packed?

Well, every time I've ever played there, they were sold out. Because if you don't sell out, they don't have you back. And every other well-known American jazz soloist sells out or he isn't asked to come back. Now I got a call just recently from Sweden. My agent asked, can you come back to Stockholm in the spring and do 20 concerts for me and we'll line up some things in 6 other countries? I've played Europe since 1950.

Do you have a preference for any European country?

Well, I love England, of course, and I loved Ireland very much. I love Germany. I'm not that much in love with Switzerland.

You're a golfer, correct?

Yes. Yesterday I played golf, and I walked about ten miles. I love that. I need it.

And you're a lover of baseball?

I am a baseball fan.

And you like to get to the track once in a while?

Yes, that's right.

Put down a few $2 bets?

Yes.

How do you bet? Do you bet to win, place or show?

No, I like to bet on the nose. You and I know there is no way to win. I think that people have a compulsion to gamble, think that there is a way to win so they follow the horses. The poor horse doesn't know. A horse that is 99 to 1 doesn't know that he is not supposed to win. He goes out and wins. Long shots don't win often enough but I've had a tremendous amount of luck in England just playing long shots.

How do you pick your long shots? Is there any method to your madness?

No. I just pick a name. I remember some 10 or 12 years ago playing in Chicago at a place called the Happy Medium and the next day we flew—it was with the World's Greatest Jazz Band—and we flew the next day to London and I went into a betting shop because I know all the betting shops there and I saw a horse called Happy Medium. He was 33 to 1 and I put £2 on him and he won by 5 lengths. When I got back from the track it was 66 plus the 2,

£68 for the bet. Look, I don't take very much money with me to the track. Maybe $100 and if I lose it, all right. It's a day out. I don't do it very often and I get sort of bored with it, even when I win. I used to play poker quite a lot. I used to be very lucky and I was terribly bored with it after a while.

I have heard it said that Bud Freeman, famous jazz musician is a ladies' man.

Well, I do adore women.

A lifelong attitude?

Yes. There is a delightful story that I'd like to tell you. When I was 10 years old, my mother who was quite beautiful, was about 30 and her lady friends were, say, 28 and 30, and mother used to give these coffee parties—served coffee and cake and I was always on hand to serve to these pretty women. And my reward for that was they'd ask me to sit on their laps and they'd kiss me. Now, they didn't know that I knew that they were deriving sexual pleasure from this. Now I think of this, you know? I couldn't tell my brother who was 8 and I couldn't tell my sister who was 12 because she would have told my mother. So I held this guilty secret with me until I was 12. Then I told the boy next door who was 13 and he said, "Oh, Bud, that's nothing. You know that Mrs. Harris down the street? She's 30 years old. I've been sitting on her lap for two years!"

Sports figures, writers, even gangsters have been traditionally drawn to jazz artists, is that not true?

Well, the great Bix and Babe Ruth were fans. Bix called me up one day . . . we were rehearsing at that time, an all-star band, we were to be the first of ten well-known jazz soloists in Europe to get a band together under the leadership of Bix and in the band were such notables as Tommy and Jimmy Dorsey, Adrian Rollini, Gene Krupa, Joe Sullivan, and myself on tenor.

This was when, the late 1920s?

This was in the year 1930 because Bix died in '31 . . . . We were rehearsing at the old Roseland Ballroom in New York. During this period of rehearsing, Bix called me—he was living on the 11th floor of the 44th Street Hotel and he said, "Look, Babe Ruth is coming over today and I know you love baseball and you idolize

him." I said, "I'd love to meet him." So the Yankees were playing a series at that time with the Philadelphia Athletics, the old
Connie Mack team. And Al Simmons, another great ballplayer
and great hitter, was in the series, of course, and he and Babe Ruth
were drinking partners. So he brought Al Simmons along. Well,
they got terribly drunk. First we met them while they were still
sober. They got terribly drunk and got into an argument and Babe
Ruth was very strong. He got an arm grip on Al Simmons around
the neck and held him out of the window of the 11th floor. And,
my God, Bix was about to have a heart attack and I wasn't doing
too well myself . . .

What happened?

I don't know. Just a drunken argument about baseball. Everything about baseball . . . .

Did anyone try to prevent Ruth from doing this?

No. Bix was hiding under the bed, and I was hiding in the
bathroom. It was the most frightening thing in the world. Thank
God no one was hurt.

Ruth was joking?

Yes. They were just having fun. By the neck, out the window . . . .

How did you like Ruth?

He could be very pleasant, but you know, his childhood was
pretty bad, having been an orphan . . . .

Always a kid, never grew up.

Right. Many, many years ago there was a great sports writer
called Grantland Rice. He was on a show, I think, called "Report
to the Nation," a radio show. It was coast-to-coast out of New
York. They were honoring Babe Ruth. It was 1927, I think,
when he hit his 60 home runs. Ruth was on the show. And they
had a rehearsal. They realized that Ruth didn't read books or anything and wasn't a very astute man, so they rehearsed him several
days before the show and this is what he was to have memorized:
he was to have said, "As the Duke of Wellington once said, the
greatest battles of England are won on the fields of Eton." And
this is what Babe Ruth said on this live coast-to-coast show. "As
Duke Ellington once said," and it just broke up everybody. They

didn't really know what to do. Music stands were falling all over. This happened a year before I came to New York. I didn't get there until 1928, when I went with Ben Pollack's band.

Who was in the Pollack band at the time?

The great Benny Goodman, Jimmy McPartland, Glenn Miller, were some of the other people in the band.

You and Jimmy McPartland were of the original Austin High Gang, along with Frank Teschemacher, Jimmy's brother Dick, and Dave North. You met the great drummer Dave Tough at this time in your youth, did you not?

Dave Tough attended Oak Park High School but he was very much in love with a girl he later married, who was attending Austin. So every Friday he would come to meet her and spend the weekend with her. School closed at 3:00. About 3:15 they would have what they called a social hour and some of these musicians attending Austin who had already become pros, would play for it. It was a dance. Dave would come over to dance and once in a while he would sit in. He was about 15 years old then and he had already become a professional player.

And you were how old?

I was 14.

This was about the time you got your first instrument?

No, I didn't get the instrument until I was 16. I met Jimmy McPartland and his brother Dick at Austin High School. We became very good friends and they were into music. Jimmy played a little trumpet, coronet and violin and his brother played guitar and they talked my father into buying me a saxophone [a C-Melody sax]. And for two years I fooled around with that thing, and had a few jobs that were disastrous. And then I changed to tenor and then I realized that I was getting into something deep and I studied with a symphonic player. I studied clarinet with him for a few months and he taught me how to read. And then things started happening for me. I got into working more but always working as a jazz soloist. I met Eddie Condon and Red McKenzie. Red was a pretty good businessman. He went in and sold the O.K. record people in Chicago on the idea of recording a group of guys who had a reasonable style. That was later to be called the "Chi-

Louis Armstrong—"Nobody played like Louis."

cago Style." What we were playing was our impression of Louis Armstrong and King Oliver. It was our impression which was entirely different from the way they played. But, we made this record and it became known all over the world. And on the strength of my solos on that, I was given this wonderful offer to go with Ben Pollack which was then the top band in the country for that kind of music.

And your first appearance in New York with Pollack was where?

At a wonderful supper club—white tie, tails and tiara and slipper—a place called The Little Club, across the street from the Little Theatre, 43rd Street I believe.

It was a fairly long engagement wasn't it?

We worked there about six months and then we were fired because every Sunday was sort of theatrical night and all our crazy musician friends would come down and turn the piano over and do all kinds of wild things. The boss finally threw us out. It wasn't the kind of band he really wanted anyway.

When you say crazy musician friends, does this include white and black?

No. In those days we had to go to Harlem to visit our black friends and listen to them play.

Were the black musicians permitted into the white clubs?

No, they were not.

Not under any circumstances?

They played in them. It was this prejudice that was just incredibly heavy in those days. I think that was one of the reasons we were not happy about working in any of these places because we felt strongly about black people. We felt they had given us the only original music we ever had. And we treated them pretty shabbily. Not we, as musicians, because when we went into Harlem we made many friends and they treated us beautifully and of course, we loved them. I think of all the years before in Chicago when I was growing up where Dave Tough introduced me to the black man's music.

Jackie Robinson was the first man to really break the race bar-

Leon Bix Biederbecke, 1923—"Everybody learned from Bix."

rier in the major baseball leagues. Who was the first black jazz musician to break that barrier? Could you pinpoint someone?

I think it might have been Louis Armstrong. I really don't have any way of knowing, you see, but I should have thought that Louie would have been one of the first.

Writers, it has been said, have been attracted to jazz artists. Wasn't John O'Hara one of your more dedicated fans?

John O'Hara had already written *Butterfield 8* before I met him. He was drinking very heavily and he was a very, very dangerous guy. A truculent sort of guy when he was drinking. He was a big man and he was a street fighter and a miserable guy when he was drinking but fondly enough and strangely enough he had this wonderful regard for jazz musicians. I knew him some time after the war about 1953; he had a column in *Collier's* and, I was playing on 47th Street in New York, at a real dive with Eddie Condon's band, and John O'Hara came in. It was a gangster-ridden place. And John O'Hara came in to the place, terribly drunk, and kicked the waiter, punched the bartender, and these mobsters were really going to do him in. I broke in 'cause I knew them all and said, "Wait a minute fellas, this is John O'Hara, the famous novelist. I can get to him. I can reach him. I can handle him." And they said, "Who'd know anybody like dat?" I walked up to John, he was swinging away, and said, "John, this is Bud Freeman." He said, "Bud Freeman? Where in the hell are you playing?" We became very good friends and he used to put me in his column and I found him to be a very delightful guy.

He also put you in a short story.

Yes, that's right. He wrote a book of short stories called *Hat On The Bed* and the story about me was the flatted saxophone or something like that.

Getting back to your youth, your early days in jazz. It was a white group, the New Orleans Rhythm Kings who first influenced you and the Austin High Gang as I understand it.

You're right. I was invited to a fraternity dance. I was 17 years old. I wasn't in the fraternity, but it was an Austin High School fraternity and they gave their dance at the Congress Hotel and they hired the New Orleans Rhythm Kings. And that's where

I went to hear them. The first time I ever heard any music quite like that and then on the strength of that, getting to know a little more, I went to hear King Oliver and Louie. And once I heard King Oliver and Louie, I never went back to the white New Orleans Rhythm Kings. Because when I heard King Oliver and Louie, I knew I was hearing the real thing.

What about white contemporaries?

Of course we were very strongly influenced by Bix, who was white. There were some great white players. All the great artists have been greatly influenced and Bix was influenced by, certainly, Louis in a way, certainly very much by Bessie Smith. Very much by James P. Johnson, all the great innovators, black innovators of that day, because he spent his childhood listening to all these people, you see? But he was also influenced by Debussy and Ravel and Scriabin, all the great modern composers.

You can see traces of Debussy in "In A Mist," Bix's composition.

Absolutely, oh yes. Bix was a genius. No one quite like him. But there were strange influences—he was also influenced by the Original Dixieland Jazz Band, which was a real cornball band. But, that's going back to Bix's earlier years before he developed. The first time I ever heard Bix play on his records, Jeanette Records with the Wolverines, he had this wonderful haunting thing that was never to leave me.

Flair and tone.

This wonderful sensuous kind of playing. There was no one like him, really. Much subtler playing . . . much more subtle player than any other jazz player, though Louie Armstrong, of course, was tremendous.

Wild stories abound concerning Bix, that he was a dipsomaniac and would appear to all the world to be in a stupor, for instance, but was able to sober up magically and play a fantastic set, in spite of the enormous amount of liquor he had moments before consumed.

Bix would have a little, maybe a tiny glass of gin and he could sip away, in his earlier years and play. But I doubt very much that he could have played so magnificently if he were drunk. No one can. No one ever has.

What about drugs in those days?

Bix never went in for any of that.

In what period of time did drugs become popular with jazz artists?

In the Forties, but I'd like to make this clear. I think you will accept this. There are hundreds of thousands of drunks and addicts living around the world, of whom we shall never hear simply because they're not in the limelight. If a few musicians, a dozen musicians take to dope, all musicians are blamed. That wasn't true of all musicians. There were a handful. It was a thing coming from the war, I'm certain.

Speaking of World War II, you met at that time a rugged character named Dashiell Hammett. In fact you were stationed in the Aleutian Islands with him during the war.

He was a super guy. In the Aleutian Islands he used to give two lectures a week on China, I think it was just super. It was like going to school. He had a lot of knowledge. Was a wonderful man and he ran a newspaper called *The Adakian*. We were on the island of Adak in the Aleutians of course, and he had this marvelous newspaper and he handled all the editorials . . . . I remember that he would favor the progress of the Russian forces, our allies, and rarely ever mentioned anything about the American forces. And, as I recall, the General of the Alaskan Command came down to see him about that. The general asked him why he didn't write of the progress of the American forces. Dashiell said, "Well, sir, this paper has a policy not to publish any ads."

Hammett was pretty solvent and getting tremendous checks from *The Thin Man*, and he didn't have to be in the Aleutian Islands, and he didn't have to be in the service. He enlisted. And he became a buck sergeant and refused to go any higher than that. He could have been a general or something, but he hated all that. Hammett used to come with us . . . we played concerts and he'd come along. He was a good friend and in fact, after the war, when I was playing with Condon down in the Village he came down with Lillian Hellman to say hello. He had been drinking

A 1940 poster advertising Bud Freeman's Summa Cum Laude
Band at Kelly's Stables, with Max Kaminsky, Eddie Condon and
Dave Tough.

very heavily. He had to go to jail but he just refused to, I suppose, give any names to HUAC [House Un-American Activities Committee].

He was standing up to a group of real witch hunters.

Oh sure. For him to go to jail was a terrible thing, because he wasn't healthy enough. I think that killed him. I think he died not long after he came out.

You're correct.

But he was a brave man. I never could understand why he gave up writing, but then again, I suppose he felt he had nothing more to write about. After he died, I got a call from Lillian Hellman. She called and left a message. I never was able to reach her. She wanted me to tell her something about my experience with Dashiell in the Aleutian Islands and I was not able to reach her. And then I went off, I went to Europe. But he must have been a great help to her.

Hammett had been a Pinkerton Detective and he worked on the Arbuckle case.

That's fantastic. He never mentioned anything. He didn't talk about himself at all. But here we were, think of this, on this island in the Aleutian Islands, with this super newspaper.

Did you know the Japanese were only a few islands away? On Kiska and Attu?

I remember that a lot of American troops were shooting at one another, five or six o'clock in the morning—in the fog one morning. They thought the Japanese had sneaked on shore.

There are captured movies of the Japanese troops stationed on Kiska and Attu. And they appear as little boys, playing in the snow, tumbling, sliding down hills, all great fun.

An officer told me that when they first hit Attu, they found women's clothing, bras and things, because the Japanese officers had their own women.

Camp followers.

Yes. Incredible.

A case of an army traveling more on its back than its stomach. What were your duties in the Aleutians other than to practice every day?

We didn't practice every day, we just played. We were paid for a lot of the dates we played.

In addition to your regular army salary?

Sure. Yes, we played the little clubs around. We were playing all the time, and then we got a show together. Somebody wrote a show called *Take a Break*. We had some very good actors and good writers and it was a very good band. And had orchestrators and so I was lucky to have that because we toured. We got a furlough, of all places, to the mainland—Mt. McKinley, Fairbanks, Anchorage, and all that. We had a ball, because there were some women out there. There were no women in the Aleutians, other than a few old women that worked for the Red Cross.

What was Alaska like in those days? Was it still pretty rough and ready?

I saw a few brawls, but those were regular Army/Navy things. It was just terribly cold. We were there during winter. It was 40° below zero. And they warned us not to go out—stay in and take it easy, or get your nose frozen. But, interestingly enough, the Aleutian Islands were not really cold, you see? About three in the morning there was a Florida-like breeze that came in. I think it was called the Japanese Current. And it would actually get warm. It snowed a great deal but it rained most of the time. Nothing grows excepting tall reed-like grass which they called tundra. And in August, strangely enough, little dandelion-like flowers grew. There wasn't a tree within thousands of miles . . . 3,000 miles. There was very little calcium and a lot of men were having trouble with their teeth. I was very lucky. An officer friend was a dentist. He took care of my teeth. The food was not bad.

You weren't eating K-rations, I take it?

No, good heavens no. The guys who went up there in the beginning did, I suppose, but I didn't get there until November 1943. So I was very lucky, really. But it's putting in the time, you see, but we had this show. We played all the . . . we toured the Aleutian chain and played outposts and people loved it. It was a good show. A good band.

Were shows coming up there?

There were shows coming, oh yes, very big Broadway shows, and USO shows.

Did you run into any of your jazz friends?

Yes, we knew them all, sure.

Was Goodman doing that?

I don't recall any well-known bands coming to the Aleutians but there were a lot of well-known actors who came up.

I want to go back a little bit after mentioning Benny Goodman's name. I understand that you never really liked the big band concept.

Not very much, no. Because I was a soloist and I liked the freedom of being a soloist. The freedom that I have today. I didn't enjoy playing in the saxophone section. I liked playing with Tommy [Dorsey] because he gave me so much freedom. He seemed to like my playing very much and he allowed me to play. And of course, in all the big bands I played, I was the soloist. The greatest mistake I ever made was to go with Benny Goodman. Benny Goodman was a wonderful musician and there was no reason why he would ever want to feature me, because he was the great reed player. And so I was very unhappy there. I left Tommy Dorsey and it was a very foolish move. But Dave Tough, my dear friend, and Jess Stacy, were with Benny Goodman and they'd call up all the time and say, "Oh, Bud, it's wonderful, why don't you come over and stop playing all that commercial music?" Well, Benny's music was much more commercial than Tommy's because Tommy wasn't selling jazz so he'd let you really play with it. Benny was selling jazz. It became very tense at times. Now Benny —I don't mean to put him down; he's a super musician, and as a young man, he was a lovely guy, a very good friend—became some sort of strange creature. He was a genius in a way and he was at the top of the music business but he believed all that publicity . . .

He was the King of Swing?

He wasn't the King of Swing. If anybody was the King of Swing it was Louie. Look at Paul Whiteman, who called himself the King of Jazz. It had nothing to do with jazz. The only jazz he might have had was Beiderbeck and Frank Trumbauer and the Dorseys. But Whiteman loved Bix. He really did. He loved jazz

Bud Freeman, at work, 1930s.

players. He was wonderful to me in the short time I was with him.
He loved jazz players.

*What was the phenomenon that really brought about the big
bands? There is a lot of nostalgia now for the big bands. You
have people devoting entire programs to big bands and there is a
cult. What really gave birth to the concept of the big band era?*

A big band was considered to be around ten men, white men.
Those were considered to be big bands. Well what was a big band
actually was like a small symphony. You had the brass sections, as
many men as seven, eight men in a brass section, three trombones,
three trumpets or two trombones, four trumpets, six or seven
saxophones, in some cases. A rhythm section, guitar, bass, piano
and drums.   The idea of the big band began when Whiteman
started to play. Whiteman actually made his name by playing the
classics, like playing many things of Rimsky-Korsakov, composers
of that era, and putting them into dance music. And that was the
beginning in a sense. Because he had the musicians who could
read anything. They were excellent musicians. Many of them
could have played in the symphony if they chose. And, in fact I
think Whiteman himself played in the Denver Symphony.

It's a democracy of music, don't you think?

Yes.

*The rise of the big bands is of the same period of the New Deal,
FDR, the great democracy and the concept of the people.*

An interesting concept. I played with the Roger Wolf Kahn
Band in 1932, that was about an 18- or 20-piece band. We were
playing for dances and playing in restaurants. There was no market for big bands yet. Maybe in some theaters where they would
play for a stage show or something. The big band era came along,
let us say, beginning in 1930. I didn't go on the road with Tommy
Dorsey until 1936. The big band era started in the East from, say,
Virginia Beach up to Maine. Now, we weren't playing for concerts,
we weren't featuring jazz. We were playing for dancing. If it had
not been for those ballrooms, and amusement parks all over the
country that needed big bands, to draw people, there would have
been no big bands. Maybe a few.

Whiteman did not play hundreds of one-nighters. He played

Glenn Miller (top) ". . . filed bankruptcy three times before he ever made it." Igor Stravinsky (bottom); "When [he] went to do *The Rite of Spring* they just about exploded."

theaters but he was a stage show. And when he played in cafes, he played for dancing. I can give you the reason for Whiteman's having a certain sound; he had a wonderful black arranger who was in the back and nobody ever heard of him, William Still, the symphonist, who arranged this thing with the banjo which created the sound later known as the Whiteman sound. And that sound stayed pretty much with Whiteman, until maybe the last ten years of his career. Then his band seemed to lose that early sound, that wonderful sound with the banjo—not that I like banjos that much—that was beautifully arranged by William Still.

The bands that made it were the bands that had their own sound. You could tell the Benny Goodmans, you could tell the Fletcher Hendersons and you could tell the Tommy Dorseys and the Count Basies—they had a sound. Those that did not, never made it. Now, Benny Goodman actually made his name using the arrangements of Fletcher Henderson, they went back together to the early 1920s. You must realize that there were a lot of big band leaders who were not good musicians. They were just out there waving a wand. But when the big band era came, you had men who played in all the big bands and were great soloists in the big bands and became names, became famous as such and then became leaders. Somebody put a band behind them. Many of them filed bankruptcy two and three times—Glenn Miller, I think, filed bankruptcy three times before he ever made it. Thousands of dollars put behind it to get the thing started.

The road expenses must have been enormous.

Yes, but with all that work on the road, they never made any money until they had a hit record, and were heard on the air and were selling out. You didn't sell out at a dance.

You did bus routines?

My God . . . I lived in broken-down cars when I was with Tommy Dorsey, getting $70 a week; living out on the road, of course, that was a lot of money in those days.

When you were playing in the Thirties and Forties, were you ever bothered by gangsters?

I played in many clubs that were run by them but I never saw anything. They were always very polite to us. "Legs" Diamond used to be at a place called the Hotsy Totsy Club in New York where I worked for a week with the Mound City Blues Blowers and I wasn't playing saxophone; I was playing a little suitcase, drumming, because the drummer was sick. He was always impeccably dressed and always positioned himself at a table where he could watch the door.

The gangsters seemed to have had an affinity for jazz.

I don't know if it was jazz, but they liked music. They'd drink and love to dance. Who doesn't like to hold onto a woman? I found in the experiences I've had with them that they were always very pleasant with musicians and, of course, why not? We were giving them something they loved and after all, we weren't butting into their business. I do not know of any case where any musician was ever in trouble or might have been . . . . I think there was a violinist that Diamond had killed, some years ago, because he knew of a certain incident.

I remember I went to play in a place in Chicago. I was I think about 19 years old, and it was a rendezvous for the boys, these sinister-looking characters with black hats and collars turned up and guns on either side. And this one fellow, Monte, Sam Monte, wanted me to play in the place. I was to play a floor show and to play for dancing. And I saw these characters there. I was a little frightened of it all, and said, "I'm not sure that I want to work here. I'd like to finish my education and live long enough to do so." Whereupon, Sam put his arm around me and said: "Buddy, I don't want you to worry about nobody in this here joint, because nobody in this here joint will hurt you unless he gets paid for it." They were always smiling, "Hi" and "Very nice music" and always tipping, of course, they tipped well. It wasn't their money. I think I remember playing in a place in East St. Louis, and the owner took a liking to me. He used to say, "Geez, Bud, you got a lot of class." And I'd have to go with him every night and get very drunk and he'd want to go down to a place that was like a brothel. They had good food down there and I had to go with him to keep him company. One night, one of the gals, a professional gal of the brothel, came over and threw her arms around me and said, "Isn't he cute?" And this boss, this tough boss I was with, said: "Get your arms off him! Get away from him! He's different than us."

You didn't even get a chance to protest the fact that you may not have wanted to be protected?

I'll tell you a funny thing about him though. He liked me. I told him one night: "The hours are just too long. We're playing here from ten at night to three in the morning. Couldn't we start at eleven?" He said: "You got it, kid. What do you want? Anything . . . ." He was so nice.

Capone was a great lover of entertainers but he seldom went out to nightclubs to see acts. He had the acts kidnapped and brought to him. He kidnapped the Ritz Brothers right in the middle of their routine. Four fellows walked onto a Chicago stage and said, "Let's go." And they filed right out, got into a couple of limousines, and were driven out to Cicero to the Hawthorne Inn which was Capone's headquarters. Capone was in the ballroom alone. He told them: "I hear you fellows have a real good act. So go ahead. By the way, I'm paying you, so be good."

There were what, three brothers? I worked with them at the Sun & Surf Club in Long Beach, New York. And that was run by the Dutch Schultz mob. I was with Roger Wolf Kahn's band there and we played their act and they were funny. Martha Raye was the gal singer in the band.

Martha Raye, the comedienne?

She later *became* a comedienne, but she was then singing in the band. She was a good singer. And one night, strange thing, after the show, a lot of show people stayed around, the Ritz Brothers and other people, and she did a routine on the Ritz Brothers that was incredible and some big agent was there—all the big agents used to hang out there. He saw this routine and, a month later, the band was no more, but she became a comedienne.

And a very big name in the field of comedy.

Yeah, and that's where it started about there. Out of that band. Some great people in that band. And a wonderful orchestra. I'll never forget Roger Wolf Kahn. He was the son of the financier, Otto Kahn, one of the wealthiest men in the world. Now, whenever we worked a restaurant or nightclub, and the owner found out that Roger Wolf Kahn was the son of the great financier, Otto Kahn, they tried to sell the place to Roger. And when Roger refused to buy the place, we lost our job. Now, here was a case, then, where being wealthy was an obstacle getting him work. That's why the thing never lasted. Kind of a labor of love thing for Roger. Roger was a very good musician and he played well and he was wonderful to me. I was a jazz tenor soloist and out of that band came many wonderful composers who were orchestrators for that band because that band played very symphonic-like arrangements, beautiful orchestra, and, those musicians, through their fame then in that idiom, went to Hollywood where they became very important composers. Adolf Deutsch, people like that.

Were you ever inclined to think that you might work for the studios and in a musical capacity?

No, I've always had a dislike for the Hollywood image. I remember the first time going out to California about 1950, I was invited out to play the big jazz festival. They had every name in the field and I hated it. Nobody seemed to be very sincere. It wasn't the turnover of creative ideas that I found in London, New York and Chicago. I've never been happy about the idea of going there and to answer your question very directly, I never had any views about playing in studios because that isn't my metier. I'm a jazz soloist. I've had about 56 things recorded and published. But they are esoteric kinds of things. They're not anything that would ever become popular. They're instrumental. But I'm not an arranger, never have been. I don't write the music. I work it out on my horn and when I leave you, I'll go home and work for an hour on the horn and practice these things and work them out and then, if I feel I have a composition, I take it to an orchestrator. I have dear friends and they orchestrate it for me, like Bob Haggard; when I was with the World's Greatest Jazz Band, he orchestrated about six different things for me. That's hard work.

Harry Warren, the Hollywood composer who died recently, made a statement to me some years ago; we were sitting in his little bungalow which was next to his mansion—this is where he did all of his composing and he had a sort of stand-up piano there

and three Oscars for the "Atchison, Topeka and the Santa Fe," "Broadway Melody," *and so on—he said: "You know, I would have been better off not composing a damn piece. I could have been a heck of a jazz pianist."*

I knew Harry Warren who used to come to see me when I played with Tommy Dorsey in 1937 at the Commodore Hotel in New York. I used to sit and talk with him, a very interesting guy. He, along with a lot of others, was there to get his songs plugged. And in those days, if your song wasn't played by an important radio show or a broadcast from coast to coast, the song didn't have a chance. So all the same pluggers were there. One night Tommy kicked them all out of the place; it was one of his temperamental things. He wasn't gentlemanly. "Beat it!" Tommy came from a little mining town. I witnessed many great fights between Tommy and Jimmy Dorsey. They had this love-hate relationship from their childhood. Their father was a very good music teacher and the boys were excellent musicians. They both became artists. They were really the best of their time. But as children, I think the father might have made the mistake of favoring one over the other and thus came the Freudian sibling rivalry. And so they were never to change. I think they were close to 60 when they died, about 60. And, they were still having punch-ups.

Heavy drinkers, too, both of them?

Well, Tommy quit. Tommy said "If you want to do anything, you've got to stop drinking. If you want to be good at anything, you want to be a band leader, there's nothing to it." Of course that isn't true to say there is nothing to it. It's a tremendous amount of hard work and you had to be, in his case, an excellent musician, and you had to be a strong man to handle men. All great musicians can't handle other men. I could never do it. I mean that I could not handle the custodianship of other people, since I have a most difficult time handling my own. If you have a band you must spend all your time in agents' offices, taking pictures, having interviews, and all this for something you're not interested in. I love music. I hate the music business. I hate what happens to the music after you've played it or before playing it.

You're talking about how it's commercialized?

Freeman's friend Willie "The Lion" Smith; ". . . We had to go to Harlem to visit our black friends and listen to them play."

How it's exploited, yes. I never wanted that. I like the freedom of playing. Now I can play what I want. I've never been actually in the competitive swim of things. I've never competed with any of the other tenor players. I have a little thing that has become, perhaps, unique, and people say they can tell that it is me playing when they hear the song; that was all I ever wanted. It was just that we all have our own individual voice . . . and if we can make a living at it, we're very fortunate. But I've never had the commercial views that most people have—the drive—to make a lot of money.

You don't like club atmosphere anyway.

When I was learning to play I worked in all these places and now that I don't drink and don't smoke, the atmosphere is bad for me.

In all of your travels in the United States, what area of the country did you least enjoy? The South?

Well in the beginning I loved the South. Then it got shocking. We played concerts for chain gangs and it was very depressing.

Chain gangs?

Yes, we played for chain gangs in Savannah. I was playing at a place, a ballroom out on the pier with Tommy Dorsey, 1936. Savannah was a lovely town and I loved many of the people, but when we played for the chain gang, it depressed all of us. Terrible to see these fellows.

These prisoners were actually in striped suits and chains?

Oh yes, chains and heavy . . . well I saw it all. Every well-known band that went down there played for them. It was incredible. On the other hand they were lovely-mannered people. Southerners had the real manners. We thought, being in New York, people were sort of outspoken, rough people. We saw the lovely manners of educated Southerners but then they condoned and advocated slavery, didn't they? I mean that was still a form of slavery, the chain gangs.

And now, the big—and final—question: Did the Southland really give birth to the blues?

I've a pretty good answer to that. The greatest jazz players were never in New Orleans. King Oliver and Louie were from New

Bud Freeman flanked by Jack Teagarden (left) and Pee Wee Russell
during rehearsal for a 1964 TV show.

Orleans but when they came to Chicago, they developed a sound that was entirely different from the music of the Southland. And no good musician ever said, I play swing or be-bop or Dixieland. All labels are stupid. For instance, one time a man called me up to play· in a club. This was after the war, the so-called Be-Bop Era. The musicians who played that style were getting all the work, and this man called me and asked me to play in a place on 52nd Street in New York. He said, "What do you play? Be-Bop? Chicago? Dixieland? What do you play?" I said: "I play beautifully."

Joseph "Yellow Kid" Weil, King Con

No other criminal in this century, at least in the annals of American crime, provided more colorful copy for the press than Joseph "Yellow Kid" Weil, who was considered, even by his own profession, to be the dean of confidence men. The confidence racket is one whereby the criminal lives only by his wits, his inventiveness, his intellect. (In prison populations, the con man is considered to be the king of the yard.) Joe Weil's wits brought him fortunes and prison terms, friendships with famous authors and newsmen; Saul Bellow, also interviewed in this volume, wrote of Weil in *The Reporter* in 1958, giving him back-handed kudos for his ability to excel in a demanding field of crime.

Small in stature, a clotheshorse, and a womanizer, Weil worked his elaborate confidence games to support a luxurious lifestyle. "Nothing gave me greater pleasure," he once told the author, "than to take a beautiful woman to a night-club just before closing, and, when all the customers were gone, hire the band and the waiters, all the staff, and enjoy myself with this woman until we wanted to leave—to dance till dawn, the floor to ourselves, to have everything at our fingertips, even though it might cost me five thousand dollars a throw. That's what I lived for."

What Weil really lived for was to successfully complete his con games. To outwit a sucker meant thrills and the hazard of detection brought excitement. To succeed in bilking "greedy blackguards," as he put it, fed an enormous ego and spurred him on to grander feats of con. It was the stuff of the Kid's fame and the making of his legend. The following profile, in part, was written for the author's column,"Crime Journal," appearing in 1976, the year of Joseph Weil's death, at age 101.

The author first met the greatest con man in America in 1962 in the College of Complexes, a meeting hall in Chicago run by Slim Brundige. This was not a hall, really, but rather a beat-up, scabrous coffee shop with a permanently besmudged storefront window where all manner of oddities, including writers, artists, political lobbyists, reporters, entertainers and just plain "operators" met to drink Slim's awful brew and talk out their dreams, ambitions and carp their woes in anti-Establishment diatribes, providing the Establishment had sufficiently wronged them, or could be said to have done so, or could be imagined having perpetrated dastardly persecutions against the innocent, the brave, the talented.

Everyone and anyone had a ready forum at the College of Complexes, from Paul Krassner, editor and publisher of the irreverent, iconoclastic and now defunct *Realist*, to Bill Smith who had run for President against John Kennedy in 1960 on the Beatnik Ticket. Smith ran a bookstore on Sedgwick Street in Chicago in the early 1960s and the author, one wintry night, stepped inside the dust-laden, paper-strewn book emporium to see Smith feeding the flames inside a huge pot-bellied stove with huge bound volumes of *Punch* "to keep warm, goddamnit!"

Smith, Krassner, the flotsam and jetsam of Bughouse Square—the small park across the street from Newberry Library used as an open-air podium for anyone who wanted to rabble-rouse (later the

Joseph "Yellow Kid" Weil in 1947, age 72; "Never send them to the river," was his motto.

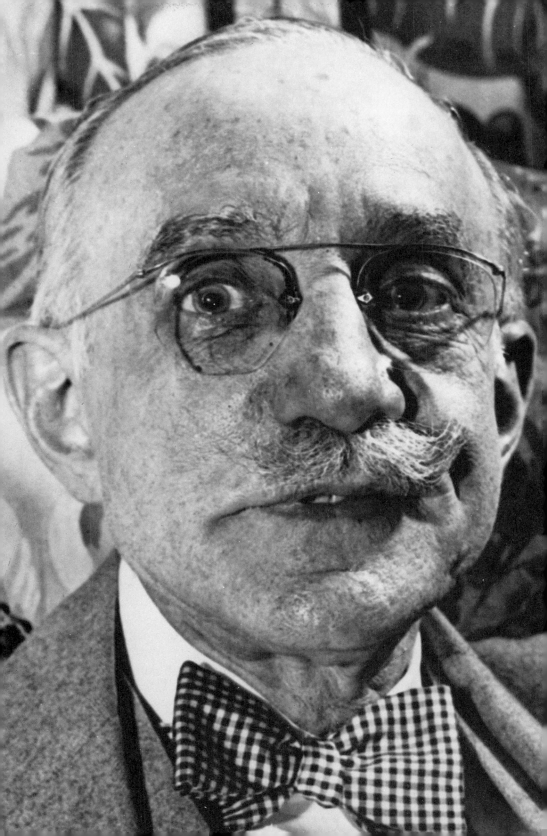

site where homosexual mass murderer John Gacy selected his victims)—would erupt from tables at the College of Complexes to deliver either a political harangue or a soliloquy from Shakespeare without a single word of encouragement from the preoccupied patrons.

One summer day, a local pundit, Jack Sheridan, was delivering some poetic ode. Seated at his table were Paul Romaine, bookstore owner, and Jacob Burck, Pulitzer Prize winning cartoonist (1941, for work in the Chicago *Sun*), who were ignoring Sheridan as they loudly discussed the problems of selling and distributing books by Henry Miller.

Puncturing Sheridan's non-stop monolog was a man who stepped gingerly through the door, appearing to have emerged that second from Mr. Wells' time machine. He wore a swallow-tail pinstripe coat, immaculate and hard-creased black trousers, white spats strapped over patent-leather shoes, a brocaded vest, winged collar and a colorful cravat pierced by a diamond stickpin. A homburg was slanted on his lion's head. A full white beard, parted at the chin and brushed to either side of his cheeks and a pince-nez perched on a long nose, behind which blue eyes stared, completed the ensemble of this elegant-looking creature. Sheridan took one look at this new arrival and stopped talking, waiting for the man to be seated and wave for coffee. The visitor then leaned on a malacca cane, his white-gloved hands folded about the pearl knob, his bewhiskered chin resting on the gloves. "Continue," he said to Sheridan and seemed to listen with rapt attention as the speaker finished his talk.

Minutes later I leaned over to Sheridan's table and asked: "Who's that dapper gent?"

"Why, that's 'The Yellow Kid,' " came Sheridan's excited response. "He's the greatest con man who ever lived." Sheridan introduced us minutes later and I listened for what seemed like hours to Joseph "Yellow Kid" Weil ruminate upon the problems of the world and reminisce about newsmen and authors he had known—Ben Hecht, Sherwood Anderson, George Ade, Ring Lardner—long since dead or gone from Chicago. Weil was then 87 years old, having been born in 1875 in Chicago above his father's saloon. Of course, I knew him by reputation, even then, as having pulled some of the most colossal scams in the history of confidence games. We touched upon his long and nefarious career and he blithely informed the author that he had swindled over the decades *at least* $12 million from suckers, but politely added that all of his victims had been wealthy persons, greedy "marks" whose unbounded avarice demanded that they be thoroughly bilked.

"I never took everything they had," Weil said that day. "I always left them enough to survive. Never send them to the river, that was my motto. You see, to succeed in my 'profession,' you must never, never be greedier than your mark. You played on the mark's greed and only gave him what he wanted, after you made him want it more by telling him he couldn't have it after all. It's like taking someone into the kitchen while you're making a steak, *one* big juicy steak, and you talk about everything else but that beautiful piece of meat, making him want that steak more than anything else and, when he asks for it, pretending to be insulted, that he would take the food out of your mouth. So you strike your deal. You give him a good chunk of that steak, never all of it. That way he's not suspicious that you have a lot more steaks in the freezer. And what do you give him anyway? Liver—if he's lucky--and he's grateful for that, and he'll chew on it, his mind so confused that he believes it's filet."

The Yellow Kid sold a lot of liver in his day, almost to the day of his death in 1976 at age 101, when the author and others were still, strangely enough, calling him "Kid." The name itself, "The Yellow Kid," came about through the rasping whim of Bathhouse John Coughlin, Chicago's political boss of the old First Ward, the Levee, or Red Light District. Weil, in the 1890s, made the Silver Dollar Saloon on South Clark Street his headquarters; the place was owned and operated by alderman Coughlin who preferred to spend more time behind his bar than in the City Council chambers.

Coughlin once found Weil laughing to himself at the exploits of a newspaper cartoon character called The Yellow Kid in a strip entitled "Hogan's Alley." The heavyset alderman leaned over his bar and pointed to the cartoon strip, saying, "You know, Joe— you're just like that guy in the cartoon, there, that Yellow Kid,

always conning people, taking their money, and making them feel good about it. That's you, all right, The Yellow Kid, and that's what I'm calling you from now on." Joseph Weil was The Yellow Kid forevermore.

In Coughlin's time, the Kid practiced all the short cons, but with creative variations such as The Pigeon Drop, where a con man and a sucker appear to find on the street a wallet bulging with money (but containing no identification of ownership) or some other valuable item. The sucker is convinced to part with "earnest money" while he holds the wallet, by then switched to one with fake bills, and the con artist goes off to find the true owner of the wallet. If this person cannot be found, the sucker is told, the sucker and the con artist will split the money. The "earnest money" of course, is what the con man is after all along.

Other short cons played expertly by Weil included The Shell Game (attempting to guess under which of three pods a pea is hidden), and Three-Card Monte, a variation of the Shell Game. In his early days, the Kid also sold a fake elixir which he claimed would cure everything—from gall stones to whooping cough—but was nothing more than sugar water. He sold spectacles to farsighted farmers that were made up of expensive-looking rims and clear glass.

Not until 1908 did the Kid go into what is known in con parlance as The Big Store, any kind of elaborate scam that often took days or weeks to complete. The victims in these instances were invariably bankers or financiers.

It was in 1908 that Weil was arrested by a vice cop in Chicago for having contracted to coat City Hall with a "waterproof" solution that washed away, leaving milky streaks all over the building at the first downpour. The cop was Fred Buckminster who took one look at the Kid's roll of bills—money, the Kid told him, that was earned within a few hours of conning—and joined Weil, becoming his partner on the spot.

"The Deacon [as Buckminster, a Bible-reader, came to be called] and I would use the banks a lot," Weil told the author after our first meeting. "We would rent safe deposit boxes and then, having access to certain vault areas, bring out-of-town financiers

Yellow Kid in 1924 at age 49; by then he had bilked millions from suckers (top). Fred Buckminster and the Yellow Kid hiding behind handkerchiefs in St. Louis, 1932, after being picked up with a suitcase full of bonds (bottom). They were released.

into these areas where I would pretend to be the bank president, and the Deacon would be the shill, the man who knew the crooked bank president, me, and we would make our deals inside the bank vaults, using them as fronts. The sucker was completely disarmed. He was surrounded by money, bank money, and he was making an illegal deal with a bank president. What could be more assuring?

"The sucker would never ask for his $50,000 or $100,000 back because, even though he discovered that he had been hustled, he could not go to the police. He had been himself part of an illicit deal, obtaining negotiable bonds or whatever we managed to sell him, and was subject to arrest himself. It was all perfectly simple."

On one occasion the Kid and Buckminster rented a building in Muncie, Indiana, that had once been used as a bank; when the con men occupied the building it still contained all of the bank accouterments—teller's cages, vaults, even deposit slips. Weil and Buckminster hired a crew of con artists to operate the bank for one hour—while the sucker, an out-of-town banker, was brought in to see a bank thronged with customers depositing huge amounts of cash, and vaults appearing to overflow with cash, coin and even stacks of gold bricks. Believing Weil, then assuming the role of the bank president under an alias, to be a successful banker, the mark easily took the deal he offered, phony land titles.

"He thought he was making about a quarter of a million," Weil told the author, "but he was only getting paper. He also thought that because I was successful and crooked—just like him—that the deal was on the up-an-up. The clincher was when I would not let him have more than a half of a million of the land deal, even though Buckminster had promised him a million. We offered him the whole pigpen at first, then cut out a lot of the pigs for ourselves. It made him angry but it convinced him that he was lucky enough to get in on a million-dollar scam. He came down to Muncie with two cashier checks for $100,000 each. I would only take one of the two checks and give him only half of what he expected. That was the convincer and that is what proved we were not greedier than our marks. We were professionals. Do you know how hard it is to watch a man, cursing you, put away $100,000 that he insists

The Kid in 1951 giving expert testimony to a committee investigating rackets (top); and in 1949 (bottom). "The sucker . . . could not go to the police."

on giving you, within your arm's reach, and let it go without batting an eyelash? Well, it's hard, my boy, but that's the sign of the true professional."

The Yellow Kid was to spend less than 10 years in various prisons for his 80-some years working the con and he delighted in telling those who wished to hear it that those 10 years were not a high price to pay for his long career in crime. He did not mention the fact that his career, which he claimed had earned him $12 million ($8 million by the author's estimation) was, in the end, a financial bust. He died broke in 1976 and was buried in Archer Woods, a pauper's field, on Chicago's South side. The author was present to see this "millionaire con man" go into an unmarked grave.

Yet Weil took an inordinate pride in his short prison terms. One story he liked to tell which he thought proved that confidence games were safer and less risky than other avenues of crime (he abhorred violence and disdained the use of firearms at all times), involved kidnapper-bank robber George "Machine Gun" Kelly.

Kelly met the Kid in Leavenworth's Prison yard one day; Weil was doing a "short stretch" for conning two wealthy widows into buying a nonexistent mattress factory. Said Kelly to Weil: "You know, I don't understand a guy like you, Kid. You go right up to people, and let 'em see your face. You go back time and time again to the same person. What kind of crook are you?"

"The kind who's doing a couple of years, George," replied Weil. "I understand you're doing life?"

Joseph "Yellow Kid" Weil was also the kind of crook who had many faces. He was not only expert in impersonating people he wasn't, but he, like Willie "The Actor" Sutton, took on physical disguises contrary to his nature and magnificent bearing in order to accomplish a swindle.

In the fall of 1967 the author was emerging from a Chicago restaurant at the corner of Belmont and Broadway. As I stopped to purchase a newspaper I noticed a sleazy-looking bum standing nearby. His clothes were in tatters, his shoes were cardboard thin and cut open at the sides, as if to allow room for burgeoning corns. He stood holding on to a light pole, peering across the

The Kid in a Chicago jail, 1939, charged with mail fraud.

street, appearing to wait for someone. Something about the hobo
seemed familiar and I moved closer. It was Joe Weil and I was
shocked to see him in such a state, having lost the sartorial splen-
dor that was his hallmark. I moved to his side. "Kid," I said, "is
that you, Kid?"

He glanced in my direction, then turned away.

He was embarrassed, I concluded, at having been seen in such a
condition that suggested poverty and the looming specter of the
poorhouse. Instinctively, my hand went into my pocket. I took
out a $20 bill and thrust it forward. "Here, Kid, take it."

He looked over his shoulder, downward at the bill, disdainful
and sneering. He brushed my hand away. "No thanks," he said in
a low voice.

"Go ahead, Kid," I urged. "Take it, it's only money."

Again he brushed away my outstretched hand. "Get away
from me, will you?" he growled.

"For God's sake," I implored. "You've got to eat. You can't
let your pride get in the way of eating, Kid. Take the damned
money." This time I shoved my hand to his front.

The Kid suddenly spun around. His beard was straggly and
stained, his eyes bloodshot. "Goddamnit," he said, "will you
kindly get the hell away from me? I'm *working*!" He was then 92
years old and still *working* the con.

Age was finally the Kid's undoing. He became so enfeebled
that he was compelled to take refuge in several old age nursing
homes, but, thanks to the generosity of his friends, especially
John Vidovic, he received the best possible care and the homes in
which the Kid dwelled were the deluxe models.

The Kid's last abode was a retirement home on North Sheridan
Road, where I visited him. On his 100th birthday I brought him a
carton of cigarettes—he still smoked two packs a day—and some
Upper Ten soda. I had selected that particular brand of pop since
it was the closest thing in appearance to champagne, which the
Kid still craved. One of the nurses poured the soda into a champagne glass and this was handed to the Kid. He sipped slowly as
we talked.

**Fred "The Deacon" Buckminster, the Kid's partner in flimflam-
ming, ended his days teaching mathematics in prison.**

"What do you think about mostly these days, Kid?" I asked him.

"Women, beautiful women," he said through thin lips. His beard was gone and his body and face had shriveled. "I remember mostly those young beautiful girls who came to Chicago from Iowa and Wisconsin at the turn of the century. Poor kids. They'd show up in Chicago looking for work and the pimps who worked in the Red Light District would tell them lies, promise them jobs and get them down into the Levee and they would drug these poor beautiful girls and then put them into cathouses where four or five men would have sex with them all night long and when they came out of their stupors they would cry and carry on but accept their fate as becoming whores overnight.

"They were fallen women, these beautiful girls from the farm states. Tainted, no longer worthy of marriage, anything. That's the way they thought then. I used to tell these girls, look, you don't have to stay in this place and go on using your body. Get the hell out of here, go somewhere else. Nobody will know. Oh, no, they were finished, they would say, and nothing I said could convince them otherwise. You see how strange the past is?" He sipped some more soda out of the champagne glass.

"Sounds like your own life, Kid. You never 'got the hell out' of con."

"That's true. I could never resist taking a sucker. Never. I tried to reform several times. I bought a hotel once and was going to be a legitimate businessman for the rest of my life. [The Martinique Hotel near Sheridan and Wilson in Chicago, now the Alden Hotel.] But then some guy with diamond rings and flashing a wad of bills would come into the hotel and swagger up to the desk to register and brag how he was such a smart operator and everyone else in the world was a dumb cluck who would die broke and at that time I would feel this itch go up my spine. I just had to take the guy! I had to scratch that itch!"

Weil took another sip of soda. Then his brow furrowed and his lips crinkled as he stared momentarily down into the champagne glass. He suddenly spat the soda back into the glass, which he placed on the table. "That's pop, goddamnit—who you trying

Weil at age 99 in 1974; "Never be greedier than your mark."

to fool?" He looked backward over his wheelchair at a nurse who averted her eyes. "I know—the nurses here insisted you bring that stuff. Champagne will kill me, they say!" He sneered at the nurses. "Champagne kill me? Why, that's insane!" He popped a cigarette into his mouth and asked for a light. I lit his cigarette and he puffed happily as the nurse clucked her tongue.

I studied the Kid for some moments. He was still alert, bright-eyed, a great mind gone wrong 80 years earlier, now attempting to survive in a body that had failed him. "I want to ask you something important, Kid."

"Good—I love important questions."

"If you could get out of that wheelchair, manage to stand up, and walk out that front door and get to the street, would you, after all these years—"

"Yeah, my first 100 years," he smiled.

"Would you, after all this time, still try to pull off one more con?"

Without hesitating, Joseph "Yellow Kid" Weil leaned close to me, his eyes bright with anticipation, excitement, and said in an emphatic voice registering delight: "Does a hungry dog like food?"

Three Chicago Dynamos And How They Ran
James T. Farrell, Jack Conroy, Nelson Algren

It was the author's good luck to have met many writers of stature and purpose while in the capacity of editing and publishing *Literary Times*, a journal of the fine arts (1961-70), a successor of sorts to Ben Hecht's periodical of the same name. (Hecht had produced his periodical in 1923-25 and had encouraged the author, from our first meeting, to give it new birth, all of which is discussed in the Hecht piece in this volume.) Among the authors I met, good and bad, vitriolic and meek, the most memorable Chicago scribes of preceding generations were James T. Farrell, Nelson Algren and Jack Conroy, and not necessarily in that order. All three of these creative talents were movers and shakers of the literary world in their heydays.

Farrell, of course, is best remembered for his naturalistic classic trilogy, *Studs Lonigan,* the story of the South side Irish street youth whose life is really a stark and bloody ethnic history of Chicago. Farrell went on to write 30 more novels, including *Ellen Rogers, Lonely for the Future,* and *What Time Col-*

lects, but none of them reached the level or achieved the popular impact of *Lonigan*. Yet Farrell remains one of the giants of Midwestern writers of the early twentieth century.

He had two successors, one more famous than the other: Nelson Algren and Jack Conroy, both of whom worked and wrote in Chicago. Conroy emerged first as the editor of *The Rebel Poet* and *The Anvil*, and the author of a great proletarian novel, *The Disinherited*, a much neglected 1930s classic, and went on to publish his small magazine, *The New Anvil*, before completing other books, many in collaboration with Arna Bontemps, such as *Anyplace But Here* and *The Fast Sooner Hound*, an unforgettable children's story that has been widely read and continuously in print since its initial publication in 1942.

Nelson Algren was published for the first time thanks to the discerning eye of Jack Conroy who ran Algren's first novel, *Somebody in Boots*, in his magazine, *The New Anvil*. Algren went on to become a stellar writer, producing books that were critical as well as commercial successes, his constant poor-mouthing to the contrary. Algren is best remembered for such books as *Never Come Morning, A Walk on the Wild Side,* and *The Man with the Golden Arm* (which most consider his finest work). A realist, Algren's chief inspiration for his work was the West side slum area of Chicago, the downtrodden, the drug-addicted, the hopeless, and he was a master at depicting the anti-social character.

Having personally known all three of these distinguished gentlemen innovators, I recall them as widely divergent individuals. Farrell was an unpredictable and colorful zany; Algren, a churlish hornet of a man always ready to sting; Jack Conroy was (and is) an affable, steady-as-a-rock literary force who encouraged and inspired more young writers than he probably cares to remember from his present-day sanctuary of Moberly, Missouri, his homestead, where he is now penning his considerable memoirs.

What follows are anecdotal recollections of personal experiences with these three writers, taken from notes kept

over the years, and bright hot memories that have gone un-
diminished to the time of this writing in December 1981.

One day in 1962 I received an urgent call from a lady who
lived down the block from my apartment on Clark Street: James
T. Farrell, an old acquaintance of hers, she said, had suddenly
dropped by and would I like to meet him? Yes, I would.

A few minutes later I sat in the woman's living room watching
the living legend of *Studs Lonigan* stand in the center of the room,
smoking and weaving as he talked through a cupped hand that held
a cigarette, puffing incessantly so that smoke rose in a small cloud
about his head, holding the cigarette so tightly with his cupped
hand that his words were muffled and I had to strain to hear.

"Tell me about your newspaper, this *Literary Times*," Farrell
said. He had repeated this line after I told him I could not understand what he was saying, but he continued holding the burning
cigarette close to his mouth, staring down at me through glasses
with lenses so thick that his eyes appeared enormous, almost gro-
tesque.

I told him about the newspaper, then asked him to write a
monthly column for the publication.

The cigarette came away from his mouth. He sat down in a
rocking chair, thinking, staring at me and saying nothing for several minutes. Then he said: "I have to be paid. I know these literary publications. For the glory and honor of art—crap! I have to
be paid. Let's understand that out front, that is, if I decide to
write a column for this paper."

"But I don't pay anyone. The advertising and sales barely
cover the cost of printing the *Literary Times*. No one who writes
for the paper receives payment."

"I will." He rocked determinedly.

"I support myself with a job as an editor on a trade magazine,"
I tried to explain. "If I pay you, I will have to take it out of my
salary."

"You'll have to do that then."

"I've got a wife and child to support."

"You want a monthly column from me or not?"

"Yes."

"Then you have to pay for it."

"How much?"

Farrell thought for a moment. "Twenty-five dollars a column."

I agreed. Twenty-five dollars was *big* money in those days, but I agreed because he was James T. Farrell. The column Farrell wrote for the paper over the years is best described as a variety column; he wrote about anything that or anyone who displeased his literary notions. The copy he sent in was handwritten, large letters sprawling across several pages. His script was so indecipherable that I wound up calling him in New York and spending a young fortune having him tell me what he had written, if he could remember.

On several occasions, I visited Farrell in New York through the years, going to the Beaux Arts Hotel where he had turned a small apartment into a disaster area. He had obtained apple crates and had stacked these almost to the ceiling to use as bookshelves. To anchor the crates, Farrell had nailed them into the stucco walls. Further, to make a larger passageway in a small hallway, Farrell had widened the archway by hammering out plaster and wallboard. That part of his apartment looked as if someone had casually tossed a live grenade into the passageway. Well, the place was "lived in."

Farrell's preoccupation with money never changed. When I visited with him in New York he would demand payment for columns he had not yet written. He was not starving by any means. In fact his novels then being published by Doubleday provided him with considerable funds, or so he said. All about his apartment were large jars and jugs and clear glass vases stuffed with bills —fives, tens and twenties. I remember asking him once to cash a small check for cab fare, until I could cash some larger American Express checks later that day.

Farrell turned from his writing desk at that moment, a look of pain flooding his florid face. "Gee, Jay, I don't have a dime in the house. I'm flat broke myself, busted."

I stared in amazement at the jars and jugs filled with bills. Not

James T. Farrell, author of *Studs Lonigan*, shown in the early 1950s (top). Farrell in the early 1960s when he was a long-distance runner (bottom).

six inches from his hand was a huge goldfish bowl jammed with what must have been several hundred dollars in bills.

"Jim—it's only for ten dollars."

He shook his head in genuine apology. "If I could help you out, I would. You know me. You can have the shirt off my back." The shirt on his back at the time boasted several moth holes, cigarette burns and assorted rips and tears.

I stood in silence for a few minutes then headed for the door. "Wait a minute," Farrell called, and dashed into his bedroom. He returned with a fistful of small change—dimes and nickels—thrusting this treasure into my hands. "I've been saving coins to buy cigarettes, but you take it."

"I don't want to take your cigarette money."

"Naw—go ahead. I'll give up smoking for a few days. Go ahead. Say, where are you going, anyway?"

I told him I was going to get something to eat and then go uptown to see a friend, another writer.

"Good," he decided on the spot. "I'll have something to eat with you." In a few minutes he had slipped on some shoes and put on a sportcoat. As we left his apartment, he dipped his hand into the goldfish bowl and withdrew half a dozen bills which he jammed into his pocket.

In the lobby of the Beaux Arts a clerk caught up with Farrell as we were about to leave. Sheepishly, the clerk asked if Farrell was planning to pay his rent in the near future, mumbling in a low voice something that sounded like "It's been two years."

Farrell exploded, sweeping his own glasses from his face. "You've got a lot of nerve insulting me like this in front of my friend here. Do you know that this gentleman is one of my publishers?"

Fear shot up my spine as I hastily envisioned Farrell demanding that I pay his back rent with advances on columns for the next decade. Praise God, he did not.

"You have embarrassed me in front of one of my employers," Farrell snarled to the clerk. "Don't you bother me again, ever!" The clerk retreated to his desk, visibly shaken, frightened. As we hurried outside Farrell smiled broadly, confiding: "The owner likes me, likes having me live here. I'll have to call him and tell him that his employees are becoming rude. I can't stand rude people."

Following breakfast, Farrell went back to his apartment, asking that I come by in the afternoon to meet his girlfriend, "an Indian lady of great beauty—East Indian." I met him at the appointed hour and we went to his girlfriend's home, walking up three flights to her apartment, Farrell chatting amiably as we trudged upward.

At the third landing he paused and stared at me. His mouth turned into a hard grimace. His hands went out to the lapels of my coat and he grabbed them fiercely, drawing me toward him. His words shot out like bullets barking from a .45 automatic: "If you make a pass at my girl, I'll kill you!" The sound of his voice had murder in it, I thought at the time, and his words seemed unusually slurred, as if he had become suddenly drunk, but then I remembered that he had quit liquor long ago and that his slippery sounding speech was the result of badly fitted dentures.

Taking his hands slowly away from me, my own hands locked about his wrists, I smiled and said, "Don't be silly."

In an instant his mood changed and he shrugged off his suspicions, knocking lightly on the girlfriend's door and saying sweetly, "It's me, dear, Jim."

A tall and darkly beautiful woman, dressed in East Indian garb, opened the door and invited us inside. She served tea and asked about Chicago. Farrell sat alone, against the wall of the large room, squatting on a big pillow and glaring at me. The woman sat alone against another wall in a captain's chair. I was against another wall, on a cushion. We had taken off our shoes, at Farrell's insistence, and I remember thinking then that he had confused Indian and Japanese customs. We all had to talk loudly to be heard in that large room and I hurriedly drank my tea as Farrell's glower in my direction deepened.

Suddenly I stood up, tucking my shoes under my arm. "Well, thank you for a delightful time," I said to Farrell's girlfriend, "but I *must* be going. Pressing business."

"Oh, that's too bad," Farrell said as he jumped up and escorted me to the door, giving me a wide smile.

Farrell's girlfriend came forward, a perplexed look on her pretty face. "But you've only been here ten minutes."

"He's an awfully busy guy, honey," Farrell told her and more or less shoved me out the door, gently pushing me toward the stairs as he closed the door behind me, saying through a crack: "Glad you could meet my girl. Too bad you have to run. See you later." He slammed the door. As I slipped on my shoes, then walked toward the stairs, I heard him bolt the door then slide on the chain lock. James T. Farrell was taking no chances.

I witnessed the tough, almost maniacal side of Farrell's personality again in 1963 when his novel, *The Silence of History*, was published. I was in New York at the time and we met for lunch. Farrell only pecked at his food, then shoved away his plate. He brought out a copy of *The Saturday Review*, which carried a critique of his novel by Granville Hicks.

"Don't bother reading that bastard's review," Farrell told me. "He's done what he always does to my books—condemned it, attacked it, blasted the hell out of it. He hates me, ever since he gave up the proletarian concept back in the Thirties."

I suggested that Farrell finish his lunch and forget about it. He went on eating half-heartedly, continuing to grumble about Hicks' lifetime persecution of his work. When we left the restaurant, Farrell led me—or rather trotted, since he considered himself a great runner—down several streets until we arrived at a coffee shop, his destination. He motioned me to the counter, telling me to "have a cup of coffee. I'm gonna fix that old bastard once and for all!" With that he made a call from a pay phone next to the counter, all the while staring out the drugstore window, looking outward and upward.

His party answered and Farrell shouted into the mouthpiece: "Hicks! Is that you?" Farrell turned toward me for an instant to see if I was listening to his conversation which he obviously meant to be overheard. "I'm fed up with your goddamn attacks. Who do you *think* it is—it's Jim Farrell, that's who. Yes, that's right. Now you listen to me, Hicks! You look out your window right now. I'm down in the coffee shop across the street from your place." Farrell was craning his neck to look upward through the drugstore window. He glanced toward me, saying: "I saw his drapes move." Then into the phone's mouthpiece: "Well, I'm down here and I'm going to wait for you to come out and we're going to settle this once and for all. I'm waiting for you, Hicks!" He slammed the receiver into the cradle.

It seemed impossible but here were two distinguished writers, Hicks then age 61, Farrell, 59, about to do battle over a book review. I dreaded to see such valuable literary blood flow down the uncaring gutters of New York City.

Farrell stood staring out the window for a few minutes, then walked outside and stood on the corner, looking up at the high-rise building. He waited for at least ten minutes before coming back into the coffee shop. He waved for me to join him. "Looks like he's not coming down, the coward," Farrell said with disgust. We walked outside and Farrell looked upward once more at the high rise across the street. "He's up there—see—did you see those drapes move, that's him, the coward! Did you see the drapes move?"

"What floor?"

"Sixth."

"I think so." I hadn't seen the drapes move and I didn't even know if Farrell had truly talked to Granville Hicks on the phone, but it didn't matter. Farrell felt better after having hurled down his gauntlet as in days of old on the South side of Chicago. Lonigan, too, would have made that phone call, surely.

That day Farrell practically ran all the way home. He loved to run and he ran wildly in spurts, his body jangling and quivering as he leaped forward. I tried to keep up with him, dashing through the crowds until I was overcome with a sense of the ridiculous. I was wearing a three-piece pin-striped suit and carrying a briefcase and I was furiously running alongside James T. Farrell, panting, my vision blurred. It was madness. I stopped. He halted to look back disdainfully. Breathlessly I told him I would meet him at the Beaux Arts later; I would take a cab.

"What? For Chrissakes, how old are you? You got to be 30

years younger than me!" (I was 34 years younger than Farrell at the time.) "And you can't keep up? C'mon, it's only another mile!"

I refused and hailed a cab.

Farrell was disgusted with me, standing hands on hips. "You young fellows are all the same—no energy, no stamina." Then he shouted so loud that a dozen passersby stopped in their tracks, turning to look at him with wide and apprehensive eyes: "You've got to have stamina to stay alive in this world!" With that he turned on his heel and dashed off in a great burst of speed, dodging recklessly in and out of the crowds.

An hour later, Farrell was posing happily in his apartment for photographers sent over from the Associated Press; someone was doing a story on him and his new novel.

The AP reporter asked Farrell: "What do you think of that review Hicks gave your book?"

Farrell's voice was calm and he said without a quiver of emotion: "I never answer bad reviews. It's a mistake. You take what you get—that's the business."

Farrell's way of doing business was peculiar, no doubt, but he possessed a certain *esprit* that made one think of anything but surrender, submission and failure. He always marched to the front like Kipling's good soldier but only to his own battlefields strewn with the corpses of reviewers and critics, at least these were the slain in that fertile imagination. And he kept running. He was running some years later when I met him at Chicago's Blackstone Hotel; he was in town to give a talk, and promote a new book.

I entered his hotel room through the door he had left ajar. It was a small room with the bed just inside the door. Farrell was lying flat on the bed wearing only his pajama bottoms. His eyes were open and he was staring at the ceiling.

"Hello, Jim."

He did not respond for some minutes, then he said, without moving his eyes from their unblinking fixed position, "I'm sleeping. It's a trick I learned from my Indian girlfriend. You remember her? Met her in New York. She liked you. Thought you were a real gentleman."

"If you're sleeping, Jim, how can you be talking to me?"

"It's an East Indian trick, goddamnit! I just told you!"

I went to the phone and ordered coffee and sweet rolls to be sent up to the room.

"I can sleep for only one hour a day this way," Farrell went on droning. "You don't close your eyes, you just stare at one spot and you're relaxed, you're really sleeping but you've got your eyes open. You can converse, think whatever thoughts you want, it doesn't matter. One hour a day is all you need. That's it, one hour. That leaves me *23 hours a day to write!* What do you think of that?"

"I want to learn that trick."

The coffee and sweet rolls arrived, for which I paid cash. Farrell suddenly bolted upright and scurried to a small table where he gulped down several cups of steaming coffee and wolfed down every sweet roll. Finishing, he stood up, rubbing his ample chest. "So you want to learn that trick, huh?" He cackled briefly. "Sure you do—they *all* want to learn *that* trick." He lit a cigarette, then crushed it out after a few puffs. "I'll bet you think I'm out of shape, don't you?"

"You look fine."

"You couldn't keep up with me in New York and you can't keep up with me in Chicago, I'll bet." He flung open the door and readied himself as would a sprinter on a track. "C'mon, we'll race down the hall and back. I'll show you what an old man can do."

"Jim," I pleaded, "can we please cut out the running stuff?"

"Oh no you don't," he said. "You think I'm an old man and don't have my stuff any more. Well—watch this!" With that he dashed off down the long hotel hallway, sprinting for all he was worth, his pajama bottoms billowing in the breeze he created. He touched the wall at the end of the hallway and shoved off, returning at a full run. As he neared the bank of elevators in the middle of the hallway an elevator door opened and a well-dressed elderly woman stepped out. Farrell passed her at top speed, almost knocking her backward into the elevator. The woman stared, bug-eyed and in shock at seeing this half-naked man of 60-some years streak past her down the hallway, his pajama bottoms beginning to slip

over his backside. The woman finally began to step down the hallway in our direction, her face blushing, her voice indignant as she
huffed in Farrell's path: "I've never seen such outrageous behavior! Never!"

Farrell reentered his room, slamming the door without bother-
ing to look back at the woman. "Don't mind that old bag," he
said through panting breath. He flopped down on the bed, thoroughly exhausted it seemed. "You see—I'm not—even—winded."

About a year later I found myself staying overnight—one night
only—with Farrell at the Beaux Arts. I turned in about ten
o'clock, taking the couch in his living room which was also Farrell's writing room. He decided that he would write that night, all
night. Having terrible eyesight, Farrell wrote his words very large
on legal-sized yellow pages, putting each page completed in long-
hand into a separate envelope, then writing the page number on
the envelope and dumping the envelope into a huge box for his
typist to unscramble. I never asked him why he followed this odd
method. You didn't ask James T. Farrell questions like that.

He kept all the lights burning that night as I tried to sleep and
he talked constantly between writing jags. At first, to be polite, I
answered, then I kept my eyes closed and remained silent, hoping
that he would think me asleep. But he kept talking all through
the night. Finally—it must have been about four in the morning—
I sat up and asked him if I couldn't turn out a few of the lights.

Farrell turned from his desk as if surprised at my inability to
sleep. "Oh, I forgot—you have to sleep six or seven hours a day,
don't you?"

"Unfortunately, yes."

He picked up a letter which had been opened and waved it at
me. "See this? It's a letter from a publisher in East Berlin. They
say they've accumulated a hundred thousand dollars or more on
Studs Lonigan, on sales in East Germany, but, you know, those
bastards don't honor copyrights. They publish whatever fits their
goddamn policy."

"Did they send you the money?" I asked, my head sinking to
my chest.

"Hell, no! They say if I want the money I have to go to East

Berlin to get it and I've got to spend it behind the Iron Curtain, all of it."

"Well, why don't you go? Have a good time, a vacation!" I fell back upon the pillow, groggy.

"What's the matter with you?"

"I think I need some sleep. Can we turn off some of these lights?"

"Yeah, that's right, you need your sleep."

"You never told me about the trick you learned from your Indian girlfriend."

"It's not really a trick—it's a secret, and you don't give away secrets." He paused, then stood up. "I'm going to do something for you, Jay, that I seldom do for anyone." He began turning off the blazing lights in the living room. And he said as he turned off the lights one by one with grand gestures: "*I'm* going to stop writing so *you* can get some sleep."

"You're a real pal, Jim."

He flicked off the last light and proceeded down the hall to his bedroom. Then he boomed from the hallway: "I'll tell you why I don't go to East Berlin to spend that goddamn money! Because those bastards would keep me there and tell the world that I defected!" He slammed the bedroom door shut in a rage at the mere thought of such Communist oppression.

Oppression was the hallmark of Jack Conroy's tough literature. Born and bred in the Missouri heartland, Conroy grew up near the small town of Moberly, close to a mining complex called The Monkey's Nest and here witnessed as a youth the oppression of miners by a ruthless management that paid them starvation wages, worked them until they fell in their tracks, and broke their strikes with club-wielding, shotgun-toting thugs. He was to write vividly of these times in many books and stories before going to Chicago to publish his little magazine, *The New Anvil*. Conroy was to stay in Chicago on and off until the late 1960s when he returned to his ancestral home in Moberly.

During the 1960s Conroy was one of the few elder literary statesmen who not only deigned to speak to young writers but

Jack Conroy, shown with Gwendolyn Brooks, at the time he received the one and only *Literary Times* award for writing achievements, in the author's home, 1967.

openly encouraged their work. He met regularly with a group of 30 or more writers each Friday at the old Atlantic Hotel (since razed to be replaced by a parking lot), where he would dig into a fish fry lunch, swag down a large stein of beer, and regale the assembled group with tales of literary Chicago in the 1930s and 1940s.

Conroy talked of the W.P.A. during the Depression years and how he came to survive through government-sponsored writer's workshops. This was how he met a generation of American writers, he said, through the workshops, meeting the likes of Nelson Algren, Willard Motley (*Knock on Any Door*, and *Let No Man Write My Epitaph*), even Frank Yerby.

"Yerby stuck around for a while then said, 'Aww, you fellas go ahead and write the great American novels,' " remembered Conroy at one of our many meetings. " 'Me? I'm going to write commercial novels,' and damned if he didn't, some of the most commercial novels in this century, including *The Foxes of Harrow*." (Yerby was never identified as a black writer on his earliest best-sellers' dustjackets—by intention.)

Motley and Conroy became great friends but the black writer, toward the end of the 1950s was oddly ostracized by young, more militant, black writers. Said Conroy: "They said Willard wrote for white people and that all his friends were white people and they made him a pariah because of that."

Algren dropped out of the W.P.A. programs early, Conroy remembered. "He hated it, taking writing assignments. He said it 'cramped' his style."

Conroy's own style has always been that of the outgoing jovial extrovert. Tall and robust today in his eighties, Conroy is a happy man, one who writes every day. He was also—when younger—a heavy drinker and a jolly hellraiser.

Conroy's drinking was legendary, even up to a decade ago. At one time, Jack was visited in Moberly by the humorist Mark Harris. The two went off to the local bars and returned to Conroy's home, happily in their cups, many hours later to face a worried Gladys Conroy, Jack's wife.

"You told Harris to sit down and relax," Gladys recalled for

Conroy recently as they sat in their living room in Moberly. "You told him you were going to the washroom and you'd be right back, and damned if you didn't go out the back door and sneak back to that tavern!"

"Dammit," retorted an indignant Conroy, "that's a lie! I *did not* go out the back door . . . . I went out a window."

The tavern in question was a Moberly landmark—owned by one of Jack's relatives—until a recent blaze leveled it to the ground. It was the site, Conroy recalled with relish, "of the great chainsaw massacre." No lives were lost in this massacre, Conroy hastened to add, but something "of greater value was destroyed."

The story is that some years back a customer too tipsy to stand was denied another drink at the tavern. He marched outside, indignant and vowing vengeance. Within minutes he had returned, stomping into the bar with a chainsaw which he promptly used to cut the bar in half before a shocked clientele.

No trip to Moberly to see Jack Conroy can be undertaken without an excursion through the town, outside of which is an historical marker claiming Jack Conroy as a native son, along with General of the Armies Omar Bradley. Then it's on to a cemetery to visit the Conroy plot where Jack's parents rest, with his brothers, one killed in the mines, another, a teenager, run over by a switch engine. Conroy pointed to the family headstone and said: "This is where I will go." And there was not a trace of despair or morbidity in his voice; in fact, he grinned when uttering the words.

Jack has outlived most of his peers by now, including Nelson Algren—"Algrenfeller," Jack calls him—who died in 1981. The truth is that if there had not been a Jack Conroy there might never have been a Nelson Algren, at least as Algren is known today.

It was Conroy who first published Algren's novel, *Somebody in Boots*, printing it in installments in his *New Anvil*. And it was this first novel that brought Algren the critical attention that led to an illustrious if not financially rewarding career. "Algren was always saying how poor he was," Conroy remembered, "but he made plenty of money on his books. *The Man with the Golden*

Humorist Mark Harris visited Conroy in Moberly, Missouri and the host went out a back window (top). The ancestral Conroy plot in Moberly which is on the Conroy tour (bottom).

ONE SHORT SLEEP PAST, WE WAKE ETERNALLY,
AND DEATH SHALL BE NO MORE; DEATH, THOU SHALT DIE.

Arm was made into a film by Otto Preminger and Algren was paid handsomely for that project."

Following Conroy's publication of Algren's first novel, Algren began to see Conroy less and less. He would later ignore his debt to Conroy altogether, incapable of showing gratitude to the man who had launched his literary career.

The real break came in 1938 when Algren, Conroy and another writer traveled East to attend a writer's congress in New York. At the time Conroy was broke as was the other writer. Algren paid the expenses for all three men, including transportation, meals and housing. Conroy smiled and said: "We weren't living high on that trip, that's for sure. It was like being on the dole."

Algren stopped the dole one night when all three writers left the congress to go to a bar on Third Avenue. Spying an attractive blonde, Algren tried to move in. "His line was awful, terrible," recalled Conroy. "It stunk, and we began to laugh and make fun of him. The girl was so embarrassed by Algren's come-on that she left the bar. Well, Algrenfeller was mighty upset with having been rebuffed. He walked over to us and said: 'Okay, you two. You had your fun at my expense. You made a fool out of me. Just for that you can walk back to Chicago, because you're not getting a dime out of me!' And there we were, stranded in New York, because Nelson Algren had a lousy line with women!" Conroy and his friend did manage to borrow enough money to return to Chicago. Some weeks later Algren, too, returned, but his friendship with Jack Conroy was ended.

Nelson Algren was not a man who kept friendships, let alone made them. He was a solitary man who grew to dislike, perhaps hate all other writers, especially those who lived in Chicago, which he considered his exclusive literary turf.

The author first met Algren at a party in 1961. Algren proceeded in short order to insult all present before threatening to break a chair over the host's head; he was escorted to the door by two bully boys. "Step out in the alley," Algren challenged the heavies. They were disinclined to do so and Algren stomped down the hallway, cursing, and kicking the walls.

It was not difficult to have angry words with Algren. In subsequent meetings we argued incessantly. Everyone argued with Nelson Algren. He, at one time or other, threatened to brain Pulitzer Prize winner Tom Fitzpatrick (who threw a beer bottle at him in O'Rourke's Pub to keep him quiet) and to thrash Mike Royko. Before leaving for New Jersey in the mid-1970s, Algren, who had received a laudatory literary sendoff in one of his hometown papers, announced to the world that Chicago, which had nurtured and supported him, was a rotten city and he never wished to set foot in it again. Period. He didn't.

My worst experience (perhaps my best, considering Algren's character) with this extremely talented writer occurred in 1963, at a party given by Ruth and Bill Rinehart at their Chicago nightclub, Jazz Limited, on Grand Avenue. The party was to celebrate Algren's new book, *Who Lost an American?* I arrived at the club with Ray Puechner (now "Peekner," one of the leading agents for children's books), who worked with me on *Literary Times*. We were early and Ruth Rinehart greeted us, telling us to "enjoy yourselves, take a seat, in fact join that man down there at the far table."

"Good," Puechner said. "Someone else got here first."

We walked through the dark nightclub, so dark in fact, that we had to grope our way to the table where a man sat in the shadows drinking martinis. There were four or five martinis lined up in front of him, and the man gulped these drinks down.

"What's your name?" Puechner asked, squinting through his glasses at the man in the shadows.

"Who invited you bums here?" came a slurred voice.

"Ruth Rinehart. Who invited you?" I asked.

Puechner held out his hand. "Why don't we just shake and start over?" he said.

"Oh, yeah?" A hand came out of the shadows, slapping Puechner's hand away.

"What are you," Puechner said, "the token cretin at this party?"

I knew by then who the martini man was. "Come out of the shadows, Nelson," I told him. "Put your face over this candle so we can see you."

Algren jutted his face over the candle so close that I thought he might burn himself. "You think you're so smart," he said to me. "What do you *know*?"

"I know we're here to celebrate your new book," I told him.

"I didn't ask for you. How come Ruth put you on the list?"

"She advertises in my newspaper. Maybe that's it. Maybe she thought we'd give you a nice write-up, Nelson. Maybe she thought she was doing you a favor."

"Who needs favors?"   He reached for another martini and downed it with one pull.

"You do," Puechner said. "You act like a louse."   Puechner was a very brave man for one who was thin as a rail, wore glasses, and never had a fight in his life.

Algren kicked a chair nearby, sending it to the edge of the bandstand, where Bill Rinehart and his band were already tuning up.

"You guys think you're writers," Algren growled. "I'm the only writer in this town."

"You sound like Jake Lingle," I said.

"Who?"

"A man who said he fixed the price of beer in this town during Prohibition and then got shot for his brag."

Algren lurched forward, glaring at me. "Are you saying that you guys are going to shoot me?"

"Don't be silly. It was only a story."

"You know, Algren," Puechner goaded, "maybe somebody ought to shoot you at your book party. Nothing serious, of course, maybe in the leg. You'd probably get a lot better press."

I laughed at that. Algren grabbed his final martini and downed it. Then he placed his hands at the edge of the table and shoved so hard that the table crashed into Puechner's chest, sending him backward in his chair onto the floor. I had moved out of the way just in time, so I was not struck by the table.

Puechner got up like a gentleman, brushed himself off and

The gifted and truculent Nelson Algren on the porch of his Chicago apartment, 1950. (Wide World)

headed for the door, saying over his shoulder to Algren: "I think I'll celebrate your party somewhere else, cretin!"

Algren attempted to get up but I pushed the table against him, pinning him for a moment against the wall where he sat.

"What's the matter with you?" I asked him, holding the table in place.

There was not enough room for him to move his elbows against the wall, to get a good grip on the table. "You sonovabitch! Let go of the table!"

"In a minute—first I want to tell you that we came here as guests to honor you—"

"Let go of the goddamn table," he repeated, struggling.

"And you turn out with insults and violence. You're an indecorous human being, Nelson." I released my grip on the table and stood up.

Algren struggled to get around the table. "I'm gonna let you have one," he warned.

"Forget it. Enjoy your party." I headed toward the door. I could hear him struggling behind me. A glass fell to the floor and broke. Ruth Rinehart was talking excitedly to someone in the dark recesses of the club. As I reached the door I heard running footsteps behind me. I stepped through the door and went down a step when an arm grabbed me and spun me about so that I was pressed against the stucco archway of the club's entrance.

Nelson Algren stood unsteadily before me, a strand of hair drooping in front of heavy lids. "I'm gonna give it to you right on the jaw," he promised.

I pushed him away and he released his hold on my arm. He sagged against the wall of the archway for a moment. "Let's forget this," I told him. "You've got guests coming any minute. Why don't you go inside and relax?" I started to move out of the archway.

"Okay, you," Algren said and pulled back a fist that telegraphed his punch by ten miles. I moved my head to the side and his clenched fist smashed into the stucco wall. He let out a yelp of pain, then held his hand for a moment, staring at it, confused, hurt. "Damn! I think I broke a knuckle," he told himself. Then all the strength went out of him and he slid down the wall to sit on the steps, still holding his hand.

At that moment, as I began to walk away, a group of Algren's friends arrived at the club entrance. One of them took a look at Algren, then me. "Why you rotten bastard!" he shouted after me. "You beat up Nelson!"

"He beat himself up," I said, going down the street.

"No, he didn't, look at him!"

"You look at him. I've *seen* him."

"Why did you beat up Nelson?" another of Algren's friends shouted after me.

"I have nothing better to do than go to parties and beat up the guest of honor," I said, but more in a voice for myself, and continued walking.

For years the story made the rounds that I had bushwhacked Algren after waiting for him to get drunk, a story Nelson Algren took no pains to correct. A few days before Nelson Algren left Chicago forever he walked into O'Rourke's Pub with a group of admirers. He stopped in front of me and I held out my hand to shake his. He put his hands into his coat and said to his friends—with a smile—before moving away: "This is the guy who beat me up one night when I was drunk."

Frank Lloyd Wright, The Grand Architect Of the Earth

No other name in the world of architecture, to this day, still evokes the keen sense of awe, obligatory respect, and swell of pride in individual accomplishment as does that of Frank Lloyd Wright. No other architect has approached his innovativeness, his structural candor and philosophy as a truly native American expression in the field. And few others could have endured his oppressive life and continued to produce as did he without succumbing to insanity or suicide.

Wright's legacy in the field of architecture, particularly from the hindsight afforded at the time of this writing in December 1981, is vast, and one that offers a distinct personality and creativity, especially at a time when Bauhaus is experiencing a rebirth. And though Wright denied any worth to the German school, he is claimed by the school to be one of its chief inspirations. As an innovator in his field, Wright stands alone, unchallenged even to this day, *the* giant in the profession that ignored and abused his genius for most of his life.

Architect Frank Lloyd Wright at Taliesin East before fire and death made a tragedy of his personal life. (Frank Lloyd Wright Home and Studio, Oak Park)

Frank Lloyd Wright always thought of himself as a man of destiny, and it was this pervasive self-image that undoubtedly shaped his incredible career. Yet it was Wright's mother, Anna, a teacher, who provided the implements that gave him the vision of that self-image nine years after his birth on June 8, 1869, in Richland, Wisconsin. Mrs. Wright had discovered and gave her son the Froebel Gifts, educational toys that were chiefly smooth maple wood blocks, cubes and spheres and triangles and German construction paper. These toys were to leave a lasting impression on Wright's imagination and perception of architecture; he was to employ a concrete block technique in one variation or another in most of his designs. The architect would later write that these marvelous toys shaped his view of the "rhythmic structure in Nature . . . . I soon became susceptible to constructive patterns evolving in everything I saw."

Wright's mother molded her son as an architect from an early age, taking lessons in what was then the Froebel Method and, in turn, teaching her children, Frank being the most responsive. Wright's father, William Wright, a Unitarian minister, also taught music, giving his offspring a deep education in classical scores. He moved his family to Madison, Wisconsin, in 1878 to open a conservatory of music. Eight years later Wright was studying engineering at the University of Wisconsin.

Wright went reluctantly to a university that did not have a school of architecture, helping to pay his tuition by working in the offices of Allen Conover, Dean of Engineering. Conover gave Wright a drawing board and encouraged him to work on some actual construction but he tired quickly of the unimaginative projects to which he was assigned, serving more in the role of a surveyor. He began to grow restless, then rebelled at the school regulations and curriculum. Nowhere in his life, he felt at the time, was he fulfilling his ambition to become an architect. It was during this period that he clung to Victor Hugo's *Notre Dame*, a chapter of which he remembered from childhood where Hugo had predicted that the "mother art, architecture," would come alive with invention at the end of the nineteenth century.

Impatient to test his talent, Wright began to badger his mother about working in Chicago. "There are great buildings in Chicago," he once told her. "There must be great architects, too. I am going to be an architect. I am nowhere near it here." His arguments meant nothing to Mrs. Wright, who insisted he finish his education. Finally, Wright could no longer bear another night in Wisconsin. He went to his father's study, removed two fine sets of Plutarch and Gibbon and, along with a mink collar for his overcoat that his mother had scrimped to buy, pawned the items and bought a one-way railroad ticket to Chicago. It was the kind of unpredictable, impulsive act that was to typify Wright's long and stormy life.

Wright arrived in Chicago with less than $7.00 in his pocket. He took a cheap room and while he applied for jobs at architectural firms, lived on doughnuts and coffee. He trudged through the streets of mud in the thundering and, to him, offensive, metropolis, showing his portfolio of drawings to any who would deign to look at them, and these were few. In the offices of architect Joseph Lyman Silsbee, Wright had the luck to be interviewed by Cecil Corwin, a draftsman who not only liked Wright's drawings, but felt a special kinship to the young man since both their fathers had been ministers. Silsbee, at Corwin's urgings, hired Wright at $8.00 a week as a tracer. (Silsbee's own father had also been a minister and his firm had designed two buildings for Wright's uncle.)

Corwin became a close friend, housing and feeding Wright until Wright's salary, at his own insistence, was increased to $18.00 a week. The work performed for Silsbee was perfunctory and without challenge; Wright decided to look elsewhere for employment, boldly going to the offices of Adler and Sullivan, for it was Louis Henri Sullivan that the youthful Wright most admired, almost venerated.

Sullivan was the reigning giant of Chicago architecture. In partnership with Dankmar Adler since 1879, Sullivan was an astounding innovator in his own right who had left a prosperous architectural firm in Philadelphia to move to roaring Chicago, a prairie city beginning to expand in all directions, one in perfect keeping with Sullivan's original concepts of structure and design, inspired mainly by his intense love of botany; he always carried a textbook on the subject in his pocket. It was Sullivan's aesthetic conviction that true architecture stemmed only from natural forms, the basic environment in which it was to stand, a belief that Wright later adopted wholeheartedly as his own.

Wright had heard that Sullivan was about to design an enormous business block at Michigan Avenue and Congress Street which would also contain a hotel and opera house. He had also heard that Sullivan was seeking a skilled draftsman to complete his drawings for the project. No one was more surprised than Wright to discover that Sullivan would see him at once when he appeared in the great architect's office. Wright showed Sullivan his drawings—he had been mindful to submit work that reflected Sullivan's penchant for ornament.

Sullivan looked over Wright, then the drawings quickly. His conversation with Frank Lloyd Wright, draftsman, was terse. As he flipped the drawings, the small dark man said: "Traced, I suppose?"

"No, sir," Wright said firmly. "All free hand."

"What have you been getting as a salary?"

"Not enough."

"How much is enough?"

"Twenty-five dollars."

"Come to work Monday morning."

It was as simple as that. Wright went to work as the chief assistant of Louis Sullivan. Unlike other draftsmen, and most other architects alive for that matter, Sullivan showed great respect for his new employee, recognizing his enormous talent. He raised Wright's salary in short order and gave him a private office next to his own. His employee never failed to please him and shared completely his unswerving ideas that the monumental forms of the past be discarded and new architectural forms be created that would provide the maximum of light, space, beauty and total freedom.

In almost all intellectual areas—philosophy, art, literature, music—Sullivan became Wright's mentor and the two shared long hours of introspective conversations. Further, Sullivan assumed the role of surrogate father to some degree, after learning that

The youthful Wright when he worked for his mentor, Louis Sullivan. (Frank Lloyd Wright Home and Studio, Oak Park)

Wright had met an attractive young Oak Park girl, Catherine Tobin, and wanted to marry her. (He had met her at a dance, had actually collided with her on a dance floor with such impact that they had knocked each other down.)

Sullivan not only approved of the marriage but, with Adler's agreement, offered Wright a five-year contract with his firm, so that Wright would have the financial security to begin his marriage. Wright, always the opportunist, asked for a large loan against that salary, stating he wanted to use the money to design and build his own home in Oak Park. Sullivan agreed to that, too, and, in fact, went to Oak Park to help him pick out the lot on which Wright would build his first home. The home, built on Chicago Avenue, was designed in the "shingle style," which Joseph Silsbee had made popular.

Irrespective of Sullivan's benign attitude toward him, Wright had serious trouble with other draftsmen in the office, most of whom resented the favoritism shown to the apprentice architect. Tall, wiry and tough, Wright thought himself physically able to handle any situation. He was in excellent shape, walking 80 blocks each day to and from work. He refrained from drink and smoking. Yet, as a precaution, he took lessons from a boxing instructor during his lunch hours. The lessons were not wasted.

A few months after Wright started with Sullivan, one draftsman threw his hat down on the floor and stomped on it, shouting: "You're nothing but a Sullivan toady anyway!" Wright immediately punched the draftsman, knocking him to the floor. The adversary pulled a knife and began slashing Wright, inflicting several deep wounds, before Wright used a T-square to knock the fellow out. Wright was then led bleeding to a hospital for minor treatment. His antagonist, upon coming to, realized his sorry position and, grabbing his drawings, fled before being fired. No one bothered Frank Lloyd Wright after this incident.

The Auditorium in Chicago, one of the most magnificent theaters in the world—the acoustics were engineered by Adler, the stage and arches were Sullivan's—opened on December 9, 1889, and Wright was present to see his "Leiber Meister" ("Beloved Master") as he called Sullivan, take his bows before grateful sponsors.

Wright himself had worked on the Auditorium, performing back-breaking draftsman chores.

It was also in 1889 that Wright married Catherine Tobin with whom he would have six children in the following 13 years. During this period Wright expanded, through Sullivan's gentle guidance, his ideas concerning organic architecture, stressing geometric form which he claimed stemmed from nature, as in crystalline structures. Wright extended these ideas piecemeal in his own house, adding one room after another. To provide his family with a great library and original art works, Wright, already highly paid, took on overtime work at Adler and Sullivan, designing his first important home, the James Charnley residence on Astor Street, right in the heart of the fashionable Gold Coast. It was an unusual building for its day, understated in contrast to the Greek and Romanesque designs that predominated. Wright followed a design of simplicity of Roman brick on a stone base that almost imitated the Froebel toy blocks he had so loved as a child. Wright's first officially designed building was somewhat cold and lacked the sweep and largesse his later designs reflected but it was, nevertheless, a startling new achievement that brought him to local attention.

Two years later Wright echoed his employer's anger at the architecture that made up Chicago's Columbian Exposition of 1893. Sullivan had been led to believe that his firm would have a leading role in designing a modern exposition area, yet the civic planners brought in Eastern architects who erected one gigantic building of basically Greek design after another. Later Wright commented: "The Fair reopened wide the case for European Renaissance . . . . The 'Classic' easily won . . . . The ambitious ignoramuses in the architectural profession thought America was captivated . . . . By this overwhelming rise of grandomania, I was confirmed in my fear that a native architecture would be set back at least 50 years."

Sullivan nevertheless did design one building for the Exposition, the Transportation Building, which departed drastically from the so-called "Classical" style of the rest of the exhibition area. The Sullivan building featured a flat roof with spreading eaves, which later became a Wright trademark, and five great arches, one

within another, at the main entranceway. This was to be the last
Sullivan-Wright project for, in the spring of 1893, Sullivan happened to see a residence under construction that bore the unmis-
takeable imprint of Frank Lloyd Wright. He asked his favored
assistant if he had been moonlighting and Wright admitted that he
had been working on his own time to supplement his income. Sullivan considered this an act of betrayal and, though he did not fire
Wright, he treated him with such disdain that Wright walked out,
quitting. He later assumed the blame for the separation but could
not bring himself to speak to Sullivan for 20 years. Frank Lloyd
Wright was a man of pride.

That pride spread itself like the branches of a great elm—the
symbol of the tree was foremost in Wright's mind when designing
residences—and, as he struck out on his own, Wright began to
develop and expand his Prairie Style architecture, specializing in
private dwellings, and there would be more than 600 such residen-
tial buildings of striking and singularly different designs completed
by Wright before his death. From 1889 to 1909, Wright designed
and oversaw the construction of 125 magnificent residences, the
horizontal lines of his houses matching the sweep of the horizon
that was exclusively Midwestern, all with open and spacious
rooms, one blending into another, filled with light, a design tail-
ored to serve human needs and, philosophically, one that expressed
Wright's Victorian sense of family unity. His own house, which
had a barrel-house for a playroom where his children frolicked and
a tree through the library roof, was a testing place for his ideas as
he changed and enlarged it every six months. It also served as an
advertisement for his talent.

The Wright-designed homes in the Chicago area—the Nathan
Moore House, the Arthur Huertley House, the Edward Hills
House, the Glessner and Robie Houses—were startling and inspired
monuments to a career that could have ended in 1909, the year in
which the great architect chose to wreck his family life. Yet he
would continue to produce magnificent structures, the Larkin
Office Building in Buffalo, the Unity Temple in Oak Park, the
Price Building in Oklahoma City, as well as the magnificent Tali-

**The Willits House, 1903, in Highland Park, Illinois (top); the first
example of the Prairie Style. (Photo by Linda Levin Ragins) The
Robie House in Chicago. (Photo by D. Ward Pease, reprinted
courtesy of the Chicago Historical Society)**

esin homes, in spite of a volatile and stubborn nature that threatened for decades to destroy his reputation.

One of Wright's clients, Edwin H. Cheney, a wealthy electrical equipment manufacturer in Oak Park, asked Wright to design a house for him which he did, a one-story building with spacious gardens and low brick walls. Cheney's wife, Mamah (pronounced "May-mah"), a college-educated woman of beauty and great taste, promptly fell in love with the concept of the Wright house and with Wright himself.

The architect, who was feeling pressured by his ever-enlarging family, his wife Catherine, who had grown extremely possessive, and enormous financial burdens—Wright had borrowed heavily against future earnings, establishing a lifelong trait whereby he pawned his future, as it were—not only accepted Mrs. Cheney's affection but returned it vigorously. He and Mamah Borthwick Cheney were soon seen motoring about Oak Park together, much to the delight of town gossips. Suddenly, in early November 1909, the lovers fled, going to Europe and abandoning their families. The sensational elopement made front-page headlines and Wright, it was thought, would never recover from the disgrace; his career was utterly ruined. (Several decades later Wright, because of this impulsive act, was termed an "immoral crank," by no less an architectural guru than Walter Gropius, who nevertheless showed great respect for Wright's works.)

Wright and Mamah kept their silence and remained in Europe. Pressed for a statement, all Wright would say was: "I am no woman's property." To support himself and Mrs. Cheney, Wright sold some of his exquisite prints from his Japanese collection and later published his large drawing portfolio in Germany. The publication of his work brought fame to Wright in Europe where his influence was vastly felt, contributing largely to the Bauhaus school philosophy. (Wright hated European architecture and denied having anything to do with Bauhaus.) All this occurred while Wright, through his actions with Mamah, became a social pariah in his native land.

Catherine Wright gave press conferences at which she insisted her husband was suffering from overwork and the entire affair was

New York's Guggenheim Museum for which Wright designed the sweeping, spiraling ramp (top). (Photo by Ed Silverman) Taliesin East (bottom) at Spring Green, Wisconsin. (Photo courtesy of Chicago Historical Society)

nothing more than a compulsive sexual whim which must be tolerated in a great artist. "He will come back as soon as he can," she told reporters. One newsman informed Mrs. Wright that the architect had registered at the swanky Hotel Adlon in Berlin as "Frank Lloyd Wright and wife." To that Mrs. Wright retorted: "If he was an ordinary rake do you think he would have done that?"

Edwin Cheney avoided the press altogether, refusing to make any comment about his errant wife or his friend and architectural employee, Wright. Ministers in Oak Park and throughout the Midwest where Wright's magnificent dwellings stood, however, had much to say and condemned him and Mrs. Cheney loudly from their pulpits. In August 1911 Cheney divorced his wife and Wright and Mamah returned to America, the architect busying himself with the construction of his new home, Taliesin, at Spring Green, in Sauk County, Wisconsin. The word "Taliesin" was Welsh, and, literally translated meant "Shining Brow." Using 200 acres of inherited land, Wright situated his superb country home just below a crest of a hill that offered a panoramic view of a spreading valley. "No house should be on a hill," Wright later explained. "It should be *of* the hill."

Taliesin, which was to burn twice, and be rebuilt, changed and altered as Wright tested his design theories over the years. It is considered by most of his critics to be his finest work, even though it was never completed, a structure which thoroughly reflected Wright's theory of "organic architecture," its connecting courts of fawn-colored stone blending as did the structure itself with the terrain, rather than attempting to rise above and be set apart from the Wisconsin woodlands of Wright's youth.

To this splendorous place Wright took Mamah Borthwick Cheney. A gardner and his son, two workmen, and an apprentice student joined Wright as he continued to improve and expand the country place. It became his abiding passion, although designs for other private dwellings poured from the drawing board. One special project in 1914 was the Midway Gardens in Chicago, intended to be "the most beautiful and complete concert garden in the world," according to its financial backer, Edward Waller. Wright designed the gardens in geometric forms with flat, jutting roofs, spacious walkways and a roomy pavillion. His son John worked on the project with him and was at his side working in Chicago on August 15, 1914, when Wright received a telephone call that struck him dumb.

Taliesin, Wright was told, had been almost completely destroyed by fire. Seven persons, including Mamah and her two young children, two workmen, the apprentice student and the gardner's son, had been killed, not by the fire but by Wright's butler, Julian Carleton, a Barbadian black, who had come to work at Taliesin with his wife Gertrude.

Carleton had been acting strangely for weeks, brooding about living in the woods and telling his wife that "the country was too lonely for city servants." He also muttered religious oaths that condemned Wright's lifestyle. On that fateful August morning, Carleton decided to kill everyone at Taliesin. He poured gasoline into the kitchen where the house staff sat eating, then lit the gas, locking the top of a Dutch door. The screaming staff members rushed out, their clothes on fire; they stooped to escape through the bottom opening of the door. As they did so, Carleton brought an ax down on their heads. He then raced to a balcony where Mamah and two of her small children sat, and axed them to death. He was later found hiding in the steam boiler firepot. As Carleton was dragged out, sheriff's deputies noticed that his lips were burned. The madman smiled at them and uttered only one word before dying: "Acid." He had swallowed a muriatic cleaning fluid immediately after committing the massacre.

It was months before Wright could cope with the tragedy, and even then, being in a dazed state, he was easily victimized by Miriam Noel, an opportunistic widow who visited him in the half-ruined Taliesin to "console and comfort" him. Wright, perhaps out of loneliness and despair, married Mrs. Noel, an act which was to bring him more pain than the slaughter of his loved ones. Mrs. Noel considered herself an artist and a literary savant. Following her marriage to the architect, she began to give press conferences wherein she informed the world of her husband's great talents, as well as her own. Soon Wright was confiding to his son John that he had made an error in marrying the woman, and that his life with Miriam was miserable. He buried himself in his work, producing a phenomenal number of designs for buildings, private and commercial.

In 1915, during a worldwide talent search, emissaries of Japan's Emperor Hirohito invited Wright to Japan to design and oversee the construction of the Imperial Hotel, which was to prove to be not only an aesthetic masterpiece but one of the most durable structures ever tested by the wrath of nature.

Wright labored for seven years on the building, with 600 workmen slaving around the clock to complete the structure. The architect was ever mindful of the earthquakes that frequently shook Japan and resolved to construct a building that was literally "earthquake proof."   To that end he insisted that the building not exceed two stories. Instead of heavy masonry and beams, Wright opted for native stone in the building's construction. Further, he ordered beams and a support system beneath the hotel's foundation to be driven into its marshy base. (Wright was mindful of several buildings that "floated" on Chicago's boggy land.) Conventional rigid framework was abandoned.

Shortly after Wright returned to the U.S. in 1923 to settle in California, he learned that Tokyo had undergone a massive series of earthquakes and fires. The largest tremor had registered 8.2 on the Richter Scale. The Tokyo-Yokohama megalopolis was demolished, with 600,000 homes destroyed and 143,000 inhabitants dead. It was one of the great disasters of the century but Wright's reputation, oddly enough, benefitted from the catastrophe.

A short time after the earthquake, Wright received a radiogram from the manager of the Imperial Hotel in Tokyo. It read: "HOTEL STANDS UNDAMAGED AS MONUMENT OF YOUR GENIUS.   HUNDREDS OF HOMELESS PROVIDED BY PERFECTLY MAINTAINED SERVICE." This message was printed in newspapers around the world and elevated Frank Lloyd Wright to the zenith of the architectural community. It is true that the hotel did receive some minor damage and that, contrary to belief, it was not the only structure to remain intact following the quake, but Wright's reputation as a far-sighted, almost clairvoyant, planner was firmly established.

In 1923 Wright could look back upon 179 buildings he had designed and built, plus 70 projects not completed, including skyscrapers in San Francisco, Chicago and New York. Before his
death at age 92 in 1959, Wright would complete more than 8,000
individual drawings for buildings and projects, including his famed
"Mile High Illinois" (528 floors) building.

But Wright's personal life did not keep pace with his professional career. As an architect he was a leading world figure. His
home life, however, was a ruin. Miriam became impossible to live
with, and he finally managed a separation, then met a kind and
utterly sympathetic woman, Olga Iovanovna Lazovich Milanoff
Hinzenberg, the daughter of a Montenegrin judge. He and Olga
moved into Taliesin with her children. Miriam, who had refused
to give Wright a divorce, demanding exorbitant payments and a
staggering settlement at times, plagued the couple, visiting Taliesin
with sheriff's deputies, screaming and throwing rocks through the
windows, swearing out warrants for the arrest of her husband and
his common-law wife on grounds of moral turpitude. The woman
made life a hell on earth for the architect and his new love—Olga
was later to marry Wright and, as his third wife, live with him for
the remainder of his long and productive life.

Miriam Wright's persecution of Wright and Olga lasted for two
years and became so intense that, when Wright and Olga fled Taliesin and took refuge in a Minnesota cottage, Mrs. Wright caused
them to be arrested and jailed on charges that they had violated
the Mann Act (the illegal transportation of females across state
lines for purposes of prostitution). The charge was thrown out of
court, but not before Wright spent two nights in a stinking, bug-
ridden cell. He busied himself by designing a new jail that would
provide maximum use of space and light.

The venomous Miriam, after filing endless lawsuits and writing
hundreds of letters denouncing Wright—at one point Miriam wrote
to every member of Congress to complain of her "immoral" husband and his "concubine"—was finally appeased with a handsome
settlement and payments. She died in 1930.

Wright's career went on but during the 1930s his style showed
more restraint, although he did buy land near Chandler, Arizona,

where he began to erect Taliesin West, its stunning walls rising out of the desert, its buildings, constructed of native stone; it was termed by Wright to be "pole-and-boulder Gothic." Actor Charles Laughton visited Taliesin West when it was nearing completion—although it, like its counterpart, Taliesin East in Wisconsin, was never really completed by Wright—and said: "Frank, the place is magnificent."

A beaming Frank Lloyd Wright replied: "Yes, I have given Arizona a voice."

In 1930 Wright began a Taliesin Fellowship whereby young architectural apprentices could stay and study with him in Arizona and Wisconsin, a fellowship that continues to this day. The pay was meager but the rewards were enormous as Wright bestowed his knowledge upon his dutiful if not slavish disciples. In addition to setting up a draftsmen's school, Wright held nightly get-togethers where he would impart his attitudes and thoughts concerning all manner of art and life, his followers squatting at his feet. He became a high priest of culture, a guru of architecture and lifestyle philosophy, and the role seemed to feed the architect's ever-expanding ego.

Wright got to the point where he would not tolerate any criticism of his work. When Ernest Hemingway questioned a Wright plan for improving the Grand Canal in Venice, the architect snapped that the author's statements were those of "a voice from the jungle." He dismissed world-famous architects, especially European, as draftsmen clinging to a dead past. He was autocratic with his students, none of whom ever uttered a word of criticism of the master after leaving Taliesin.

A visitor being shown through Taliesin West by Wright was shocked to see the architect stop at the drafting table of one apprentice, look over an elaborate design, and then disdainfully draw a pencil line across it. Wright walked off as the visitor looked at the apprentice. "Oh, he always does that," explained the apprentice, and then began to easily wipe the pencil mark off the drawing, confiding that he always took the precaution of applying three coats of wax to his work.

Christmas, Easter and Wright's birthday were the most festive

Frank Lloyd Wright at Taliesin West toward the end of his life. (Frank Lloyd Wright Home and Studio, Oak Park)

times at the Taliesins; theatrical and operatic performances were given and distinguished visitors from all parts of the world attended. Wright's birthday became *the* event after a number of years. On these occasions the students would present the master with "birthday boxes" which contained designs that had taken them months to complete; the boxes themselves were of elaborate and inventive designs. Wright would inspect these "birthday boxes" with the air of Kublai Khan looking over new treasures brought to his court, casually sifting and sorting the designs without comment.

Wright's own work increased with intensity. He designed the spiral ramp for the Guggenheim Museum in New York in 1943 but did not witness its construction for 14 years. He designed the wonderful Falling Water dwelling in Mill Run, Pennsylvania, and the Johnson Wax Company's administrative building in Racine, Wisconsin, with its towering pillars flaying out to support a solid skylight roof. He continued to promote his idea for a skyscraper so large that it could hold the entire work force of Chicago, thereby eliminating the need for any other skyscrapers in the Loop which could then be turned back into a community of parks and family dwellings. The "Mile High Illinois" building was designed by Wright and followed the pattern of a giant tree where people worked on its branches, its core providing the heating and cooling systems. It was never built, except in the motion picture, *The Fountainhead*, based on Ayn Rand's novel. Wright saw this film, based upon his own character of unrelenting individualism but was unimpressed. In fact he was irritated that the film's producers had employed designs that mimicked his own.

In the last 15 years of his life, Wright's stature was supreme. He had lived out his ambition to establish a wholly American style of architecture (albeit some claimed he had borrowed heavily from the Incan and Mayan cultures). And, before he died of a heart attack on April 9, 1959, at Taliesin West, the great iconoclast uttered his own epitaph, stating that the greatest architect was one who acted "as savior of the culture of modern American society." No one dared to argue with him then. Few in the field with which his name has become synonymous dare to challenge that statement today.